194

Living in the Bush...

1946 –
Living in the Dash!

The Journey so far
Serving an Extraordinary God

Fred Merry

1946 –
Living in the Dash!
by Fred Merry

© Fred Merry 2018

For book orders please contact fred@fredmerry.plus.com

The moral right of the author has been asserted according to the
Copyright, Designs and Patents Act 1988.

Scripture taken from the New King James Version.
Copyright © 1982 by Thomas Nelson, Inc. Used by permission.

A catalogue card for this book is available from the British Library.

ISBN: 978-1-9996788-4-5

Printed and bound in Great Britain by
TJ International, Padstow, Cornwall

Foreword

It is an honour for me to write this foreword on behalf of my dear friend and brother in the Lord, Fred Merry.

Since I have known Fred I have recognised the call of God upon his life and the call to the lost, which beats within his heart like a fire.

It has been so refreshing to see this in him, reaching out as he does to the lost, at every available opportunity.

Truly Jesus said to the apostles I will make you fishers of men, and Fred is truly a fisher of men. His book has many stories that shows the Lord's hand upon him, as he is led to speak to men and women concerning their condition and their future, whether in the Kingdom of God, or not.

We owe it to the lost, as Fred sees himself, showing the lost what he has found to be his greatest treasure, Jesus Christ.

Jesus is man's salvation and Fred has spent his life giving the gift that he has received, to others.

May we all learn from his life what it is to give the message of salvation to others.

PASTOR DEREK GITSHAM. WORCESTER

Preface

I give all the glory to my Lord and Saviour, Jesus Christ who is faithful and has been constantly with me, despite my failings and kept me through the storms and valleys. I have written this book so you can know that God knows each one of us and that we can call Him Father. He loves us and He has an amazing plan for our lives. There is one who would destroy us. Jesus said, "The thief does not come except to steal, and to kill, and to destroy. I have come that they may have life, and that they may have it more abundantly." (John chapter 10, verse 10.)

In the writing of this book I acknowledge the support that I have had from my wife, Mary who is the greatest friend that I have on the earth and I honour her for her love and companionship over the years. I also acknowledge the great help and encouragement with the editing of this book, which I have been given both from my wife, Mary and also from Pastor Derek Gitsham.

I am indebted for the encouragement of the Reverend Daniel Cozens of Through Faith Missions, and all the myriad people of that organisation and also for the Seamen's Christian Friend

Society, who allowed me the privilege of being employed by them, and all the support that they gave me.

Also the inspiration of great men of God like Dr. Billy Graham, who is now with the Lord and Reinhard Bonnke.

There has been another amazing move of God throughout Wales and the United Kingdom. Be open to believe God and know that you can have a relationship with Him. Be prepared to trust Him and obey Him.

"Did not our hearts burn within us while He talked and while He opened the Scriptures to us." (Luke 24, verse 32.)

Contents

CHAPTER ONE

The Early Years

I was born in the East End of London on 29th March 1946. I had three siblings, an elder sister and two younger brothers. I spent my early childhood at a Primary and Junior school in Hackney and London Fields. I passed the 11 plus and attended a Grammar School in Bethnal Green, London.

My parents were on a low income and they were unable to spend money on taking us out. My knowledge of the world was limited to Victoria Park, Hackney, but a man from a Sunday School, that I attended, used to take my younger brother and I out, to the museums and places of interest in London.

At the age of nine, I was given my first bible by this man from Sunday School and he wrote in it the scripture reference of Proverbs, chapter 3, verses 5 & 6. (*Trust in the Lord with all your heart and lean not on your own understanding. In all your ways acknowledge Him and He will direct your paths.*)

I did not understand at that time that the Christian faith is about having a relationship with the living God.

My parents purchased a house in Gravesend, Kent and our family moved there in 1958.

I also remember my parents buying a television. It had a 14-inch screen and was only in black and white, not colour.

When I was a child there was no telephone inside the house. If we wanted to use the telephone, we had to go outside to one of the red telephone boxes and put four old pence into the coin box, dial the number and press button A. Now we all have mobile phones.

The advance of scientific development throughout my lifetime has been amazing. Science does not disprove the bible, it shows that there is a God who created this wonderful universe for us, for us to enjoy, for His praise and glory.

I had passed the eleven plus in London and attended a Grammar school with a red uniform, but the school that I went to in Kent had a dark blue uniform. I stood out like a sore thumb. I had to wait a year before my parents could afford the replacement uniform. I was set back in my school work and I was unable to catch up.

I left the school after staying on until my sixteenth birthday. I still did not have any exam credits, but I managed to get a job at a chemicals firm in Dartford.

After leaving school I attended a college and gained a couple of O levels in Chemistry and English, by studying at evening classes in College.

My sister was going to a church and she invited me to go with her. (I had discovered that there were girls at the Church youth club, which was a good incentive for me to go to the church.)

While I was there I met a girl and we later married, when I was nineteen. I thought that everything was perfect, but I did not know that I was about to have my dreams shattered. My world was about to crumble. I was divorced within four years. I was a proud man and I had failed. I had become an active member of that church and I served there as an altar boy. I could not believe in a God of love, who would allow so much pain and suffering, so I walked away from the church and religion.

I was to later realise that it was my fault that the marriage had failed, and that God is faithful and Jesus Christ never left me.

It was now January 1969 and I started employment with an Insurance Company. I remember this year well because of the continuing advances in science, for example, the development of space travel, which have been amazing and on the 20th June 1969 the Apollo 11 spacecraft took the first men to land on the Moon.

In January 1974 I left the Insurance Company to set up my own business as an Insurance Consultant. I was held in high regard by some Insurance Underwriters and had delegated authority on motor and insurance cover.

During the years that I was on my own I took up the hobby of marshalling at motor-race meetings. This was thrilling for me and I was track-side at Brands Hatch, Snetterton, Dover and many smaller race tracks. I marshalled at events from Formula 6, through banger racing, stock cars, hill climbs, Formula Ford, and Formula 2000 cars.

I was elected Chief Marshal for Rochester Motor Club for two years running and I also marshalled at motorcycle meetings and Brands Hatch Racing Driver Training Sessions. I spent most Sundays at the track, but I was to find an even greater excitement as I grew closer to the Lord.

CHAPTER TWO

Tears Turned to Joy

In the years to come, after fifteen years of being on my own, (in what I describe as my wilderness period), I was to meet and fall in love with a lady. I wanted to marry her, but I felt that I had to make my vows before God.

I had two insurmountable problems. I had walked away from God and as I believed at the time, I was unacceptable to the church, because I was divorced. In this hopeless state, I came before the Lord and I offered what I was, to Him. Because the Lord is faithful, He took me as I was.

Suddenly Jesus Christ became real to me. I discovered that He had never left me.

I went to visit a minister at a church where my father's ashes were interred. The minister there showed us tremendous empathy and he said that he would give Mary and I a good service.

On 14th April 1984, Mary and I went to the Register Office and we were married. (The triumph of hope over experience.

In 2018 Mary and I celebrated our thirty fourth year of marriage.)

Immediately following the Register office ceremony we went to the Church and we were given a marriage blessing in which we were able to make our vows before God. We were also given a tape recording of the ceremony as a wedding gift. We joined that church and I was to sing in the choir at many weddings. We found that the service we were given was a marriage service and this was confirmation that God had accepted us.

Mary had two daughters from her previous marriage and it was a great honour and privilege for me to be able to adopt them. I found out an incredible fact about adoption, is that when the court awards the adoption, a certificate is given and shows the adoptive father as the child's father. The adoptive child also has legal rights to benefits from being a family member. There is an incredible spiritual similarity that occurs when we accept Jesus Christ as our Saviour, and what He did for us by going to the cross to pay the price for our sin, our disobedience.

(John chapter 3, verses 14–16.)
"And as Moses lifted up the serpent in the wilderness, even so must the Son of Man be lifted up, that whoever believes in Him should not perish but have eternal life. For God so loved the world that He gave His only begotten Son, that whoever believes in Him should not perish but have everlasting life. For

God did not send His Son into the world to condemn the world, but that the world through Him might be saved."

(John chapter 14 verses 1–6.)
"Let not your heart be troubled; you believe in God, believe also in Me. In My Father's house are many mansions; if it were not so, I would have told you. I go to prepare a place for you. And if I go and prepare a place for you, I will come again and receive you to Myself; that where I am, there you may be also. And where I go you know, and the way you know." Thomas said to Him, "Lord, we do not know where You are going, and how can we know the way?" Jesus said to him, "I am the way, the truth, and the life. No one comes to the Father except through Me."

We also, are adopted by God and we inherit the amazing benefits of being able to call God our Father. We become His children and we are members of His family. We can speak to God at any time. We will be with Him for eternity.

My father died on 15th December 1982. My dad and I argued a lot when I was younger, but when he was ill and in hospital I found that we became closer. We had not understood that we had our own identities and that I had grown into an adult. I also discovered that my dad was a really brave man as he fought four types of cancer. I pray that he found the Lord before he died.

On 4th May 1985 Mary gave birth to our youngest daughter. Life was very good. I had a wonderful wife and I was now a father to three beautiful daughters and we needed a bigger home. So in November 1985 we moved into our bungalow. I continued to work at my business as a self-employed Insurance Consultant.

CHAPTER THREE

A Step of Faith

In 1989, Gravesend Churches joined together with a satellite link to Dr. Billy Graham's Mission 1989. I had volunteered my services as a counsellor. The Lord was gracious and the first night I prayed with a man who had re-dedicated his life to Christ. I met this man a number of years later and I found that he was now a director of a Christian Radio Station. As the week progressed I was able to support and encourage each person that I was given to counsel.

I was keen to learn more and grow in my walk with the Lord. I had heard about the Developing Ministries Programme and Faith and Ministries Course, with the Anglican Church and in 1989, I enrolled for training as a Diocesan Evangelist. This was going to prove to be another great test of my faith.

The course was a five year part time course, and after nearly completing the course, I was told in January 1995 that I was not going to be commissioned in the April of that year. I said that I accepted their decision, but did not agree with it and so I was asked to stay on another year, when I was then commissioned in September 1996.

CHAPTER FOUR

The Testing of Faith – A Spark is Ignited

Pennine Way Walk 1990

I began to have my faith tested further when I heard about The Walk of 1000 Men. (Through Faith Missions. Coton, Cambridge, CB3 7PL. Walk of 1,000 Men.)

After a period of training (both spiritual and physical) I joined a team of ten men for part of the Pennine Way Walk, from Saturday 2nd May to Sunday 2nd June.

I joined the group of nine other men on a Friday evening. Arriving at Cornholme Church in Todmorden, we had no food. We had vowed to live by faith and had only £2 per day expenses, which was to buy someone a drink, when we went into the pubs to talk about our faith. "Give us this day our daily bread," we prayed. Ten minutes later a box of food was handed in to us. Praise the Lord for His grace and mercy.

We later visited a local pub and as we were singing hymns outside we were given our breakfast. The eggs, which were thrown at us missed, but we were beginning to realise that we needed to be more specific in our prayer requests.

The rest of the team had begun to make their way back to the church and as we followed them we met two young ladies, who asked if all the thousand men were coming past that evening. (We all wore sweatshirts with the Walk of 1,000 Men logo emblazoned on them.) Having explained what the walk was about, they were asked if they knew Jesus Christ as their Lord and Saviour.

They asked how this was possible and we explained how Jesus had died for our sin, because of our disobedience to God we therefore need to repent and say sorry to God for our sins, because in Romans chapter 3, verse 23, the bible says "for all have sinned and fall short of the glory of God."

Also in Romans chapter 6, verse 23, the bible states, "For the wages of sin is death, but the gift of God is eternal life in Christ Jesus our Lord, and also in Romans chapter 10, verse 13, "whoever calls on the name of the Lord shall be saved."

We also have to thank Jesus for what He did for us, dying on the cross in our place and we need to ask Jesus to come into our lives.

We can do this because Jesus Christ went to the cross and died in our place. He rose from the dead on the third day. We also explained that Jesus said that we must be born again.

John chapter 3, verse 3. Jesus said, "Unless one is born again he cannot see the Kingdom of God"

One of the ladies asked what being born again meant. We explained that this was turning away from our old way of life and asking Jesus into our lives. She wanted to pray to be born again and we led her in a prayer to receive Jesus as her Lord and Saviour.

We discovered that her family had been following a religion and had no idea that the Christian faith is a relationship with the living Lord Jesus Christ. We then returned to the church, rejoicing along with all the angels in heaven.

This was an example of how the Lord led us and spoke to us that day, showing us who we should speak to and pray with.

On the Monday we walked to the Pennine Way via Mankinholes, heading southwards, eventually arriving at the White House Public House. We were given a lift to Ashton-under-Lyne and joined a prayer meeting at the Endeavour Christian Fellowship.

We had our meal and went out to one of the local public houses to share the gospel. That night we were invited to stay with some of the local families. Bliss. A soft comfortable bed. If you think that church pews are hard, try sleeping on the floor!

As I left the house the next morning I had an insane desire to throw my pipe and tobacco into the dustbin. I was learning obedience! I went back to join the others from the group. When I told them, they fell around laughing. They told me that they had been praying for me and when the other smoker joined us, he told us that he had thrown his cigarettes away. So I joined the others rolling around the floor, laughing. God is good.

This is yet another example of how the Lord will use us if we are obedient and if we are willing to be obedient to Him.

We had a day of questionnaires where we were asking people questions on life and belief, doing door-to-door work. The next day I met a man that I will call Len. He was reading one of the Walk notices and I shared with him my faith and belief in God and His goodness, and how my faith is based on what is written in the Bible. I gave him a leaflet and asked if he would like to come to a meeting later. He said no and went off into the market.

A short while later he returned with a plaque with John chapter 14, verse 6, Jesus said, "I am the way, the truth and the life. No one comes to the Father except through Me," embroidered on it. Len said that he wanted to give this to me, because what I had said had bought him back to the Lord. I gently explained that I could not receive it for myself, because it was the Lord speaking to Len through His Holy Spirit and that I was only a vessel. I said that I would arrange to have it put in one of the local churches. I then asked Len if there was anything else that I could do for him. Len said that he was very ill and that he was dying and that he wanted release from pain and suffering. I prayed with him for healing and peace and Len went on his way.

I took the plaque to the Walk of 1,000 Men organisers and arranged for it to be given to a local church.

I was returning to get a cup of coffee when I again saw Len, who walked up to me. He was now standing upright and he asked if I could spare him some time. I got him a cup of tea and he explained that he had been in constant pain, day and night, for the past seven months, but as we prayed the pain went!

Our God is Awesome!

Len had come back to thank God, so I offered a prayer of thanksgiving. Len also said that he had been unable to attend Church because of the pain and that he had rejected God. He felt that having rejected God, God had rejected him. I explained that God is faithful and He never rejects us and that is the reason why Jesus came to this earth to die in our place, so that we may have life and have it more abundantly.

(John chapter 10 verse 10.)
Jesus said, "The thief does not come except to steal, and to kill, and to destroy. I have come that they may have life, and that they may have it more abundantly."

We have to accept God's grace and be willing to be obedient to Him.

I went back to the town for door–to-door work and the teams returned to Endeavour Christian Fellowship, for tea. After tea, two of us were assigned to go and pray for a lady who was 87. It turned out that she ended up praying for us and reviving us! We left our host families with a few hugs and tears the next morning and we were transported to Snake Pass and walked the Pennine Way to Edale.

From there we were taken to Mossley. The area seemed to be cold to the gospel message. We prayed.

On the Saturday morning there was an open-air praise service at the George Lawton Centre. There was an air of expectancy. It was difficult to explain. We went to Abney Church for our lunch and our team had door-to-door work for the afternoon. In the evening we returned to the George Lawton Centre for a prayer and praise evening. The gospel was preached and suddenly people began to know the presence of the Holy Spirit. Many committed their lives to the Lord and also received healing. HalleluYah!

We again experienced the power and presence of God's Holy Spirit as we reached out to the community around us. Having had my faith stretched, I wanted to see more of God in action.

CHAPTER FIVE

God in the Town

Mission Bradford June 1992

The team was based at St. Luke's Church on the Fagley estate. We were invited to go on a coach trip to Filey on the East coast. On the coach I spoke with a lady whose friends had mentioned that she had a problem that she was unwilling to divulge. I prayed with her and left the matter in the hands of the Lord. A week later I saw her and she was crying, so I prayed with her further. Some months later I received a phone call from this lady, who told me that she was a widow and her son had suffered from a nervous breakdown and had lost his job. When she had arrived home after I had prayed with her, he had started to recover his confidence. Within a week he had applied for a job, which he was successful in getting and had gone from strength to strength.

Praise the Lord!

(This is another example of how God showed His grace, giving us discernment and an opportunity to pray with someone).

God's grace was also evident when I met a man who was in a hospital in Bradford, diagnosed with terminal cancer and the doctors had given him six months to live. I prayed for the grace to quietly share my faith. The man had explained his situation to me and while I was visiting him he had been taken to have an x-ray. While I was waiting for him to return from the x-ray, I was spending the time in prayer. I had a picture of the x-ray department calling him back because the x-ray was clear. I did not have the courage to share this with the man. On his return I left him a booklet, "Knowing God Personally." I went back to join the team and shared my experience with them. I was told that I had to sort out my lack of courage, with the Lord.

After a night with little sleep, I came to the knowledge that I was withholding God's truth, because I was afraid of how my fellow man might react. I went back to visit the man, who I discovered had now been discharged and had returned home. I told him of my vision and he smiled and said that he had eaten the first solid food in months. He had read the booklet and received Jesus as his Lord and Saviour.

I know that we will meet again in heaven, if not before.

I had another opportunity to stretch my faith when my mother died on 25th July 1992. One of my brothers was with me when she died. A nurse from India said that my mother's body would be taken across to the mortuary and she would arrange to have the windows left open, so my mother's spirit could be set free.

I was able to show her that this was my mother's earthly body, and she was now with Jesus, because she believed that Jesus had died for her. I read to the nurse the passage from St. Luke's Gospel, where the penitent thief asks Jesus to remember him when He came into His kingdom and Jesus Jesus answered him by saying, "Today, you will be with Me in paradise."

(Luke chapter 23, verses 38–43.)

And an inscription also was written over Him in letters of Greek, Latin, and Hebrew: THIS IS THE KING OF THE JEWS. Then one of the criminals who were hanged blasphemed Him, saying, "If You are the Christ, save Yourself and us." But the other, answering, rebuked him, saying, "Do you not even fear God, seeing you are under the same condemnation? And we indeed justly, for we receive the due reward of our deeds; but this Man has done nothing wrong." Then he said to Jesus, "Lord, remember me when You come into Your kingdom." And Jesus said to him, "Assuredly, I say to you, today you will be with Me in Paradise."

This is God's promise for all believers who believe that Jesus Christ has died for them and that He rose again on the third day and that they have confessed their sins and their disobedience to Him and have asked Him for forgiveness and that they have asked Him to come into their lives and make them the person that He created them to be.

CHAPTER SIX

Walk Cornwall
4th September–17th October 1993

Again, I saw God in action as we stepped out in faith. I arrived at Holy Trinity Church in Newquay and after registration went on to Tresillian. There was a tent meeting here and I went to a local pub and shared my faith with some men. On Sunday there was a joint Anglican/Methodist service in the chapel. The afternoon was spent on a hike to Nairns Head and there was an evening prayer and praise meeting in the Mission tent.

The next day was spent on door-to-door work. I had a good conversation with one man, who received Jesus as his Lord and Saviour.

(John chapter 1 verses 12–13.)
"But as many as received Him, to them He gave the right to become children of God, to those who believe in His name: who were born, not of blood, nor of the will of the flesh, nor of the will of man, but of God."

We held a coffee evening at a house. The next day we went to a local church service and spent the rest of the day on questionnaires.

There was an evening praise and worship service in the tent. A man came forward to rededicate his life to the Lord and we prayed together. There had previously been a family involvement in a non-Christian organisation, and I thanked the Lord for this man's healing, through his confession and renouncing of the vows made to this organisation.

(The bible warns us that there are many religious groups who are not Christ centred, so we have to be aware. Some people, whose parents follow other god's, allow a foothold for the devil to attack. This also has an effect on the children.)

(Exodus chapter 34, verse 7.)
"Now the Lord descended in the cloud and stood with him there, and proclaimed the name of the Lord. And the Lord passed before him and proclaimed, "The Lord, the Lord God, merciful and gracious, long-suffering, and abounding in goodness and truth, keeping mercy for thousands, forgiving iniquity and transgression and sin, by no means clearing the guilty, visiting the iniquity of the fathers upon the children and the children's children to the third and the fourth generation."

(Matthew chapter 7, verse 21.)
"Not everyone who says to Me, 'Lord, Lord,' shall enter the

kingdom of heaven, but he who does the will of My Father in heaven."

(Matthew chapter 18, verses 2, 3.) Then Jesus called a little child to Him, set him in the midst of them, and said, "Assuredly, I say to you, unless you are converted and become as little children, you will by no means enter the kingdom of heaven."

The next day we left Tresillian to go to Trispen, where we met up with some other walkers and went on to Newquay and signed on at St. Michaels Church. I spent the evening at Hedra Park Caravan Club. I found that there was great opposition and this atmosphere was also very noticeable the next day as well. I went leaflet dropping and met a lady who had been prayed for the previous evening. She offered thanks and encouragement.

I was staying at a vicarage in Pendeen where the group that I was with met up with a homeless man that I will call Bill. He was trying to get to Penzance and a local Christian offered to take him in his car. I went with them and we ensured that the man was safe at the Hostel in Penzance. I later received a letter from him to say that he was trying to walk more closely with the Lord and also that he now had a permanent address.

I signed up for a number of other smaller missions with Through Faith Missions. These included the Hainault and

Chigwell Mission and The God Knows Mission. I also went on The Key to Life Mission in 1995.

There were a number of contacts made and opportunities to encourage many people, but there were also times that people showed absolutely no response to God's love.

In September 1995 I joined the Walk Ulster mission. There had been a recent history of violence and terrorism in Northern Ireland, but a cease-fire had been announced. The team that I was placed in, walked along the Shankhill Road, through the peace line into the Falls Road and then along the Antrim Road where a greengrocer offered us a box of oranges. We went to Ballyhenry for the commissioning service and our team was transported to Londonderry, with a reception by the mayor and Church leaders.

We were taken to just outside Coleraine, where again we were welcomed in to a reception with the mayor at the town hall, which had just been rebuilt and refurbished after it had been bombed. It was an honour to be the first official visitors after the restoration. We walked on to Killowen Parish Church.

On the Sunday at the Church, one walker gave his testimony, another read the lesson and later we visited Magilligan Prison where I spoke about the Walk.

Four of us went on to Ballykelly Church where three team members lead the prayers and one preached. The whole team went to Killowen Parish Church in the evening.

The next two days we were on door-to-door work and on the Monday evening we had another visit to Magilligan Prison. On our return we were rewarded with a spectacular view of another of Father's masterpieces, the Mourne Mountains and Lough Foyle and Donegal.

On Tuesday some of the team visited the schools and I went door-to-door and had some home visits. In the evening we had a main meeting at Coleraine town hall. The next day we walked on to Port Rush. When we arrived there was no food, so we prayed the Lord's prayer. A local clergyman came and gave us a gift to buy some food. HalleluYah! Praise the Lord for His provision. Some of the group used this provision to buy some fish and chips for the team.

I telephoned Mary and she told me her father was praying for the team. I sent him a postcard with John chapter 14, verse 6. Jesus said to him, "I am the way, the truth, and the life. No one comes to the Father except through Me." Mary told me that her father was suffering with palpitations and he was very weak.

That evening, I went to share the gospel in a local pub. I met with some opposition and later played a game of pool and to my amazement God used this opportunity, because I won. I was able to share the gospel with the man and I gave him the booklet "Knowing God Personally."

During the night I had a picture of a lamb caught in the bramble and our Lord picking up the lamb, and its heartbeat returned to a normal pace, as it felt safe. I wrote to Mary and shared this picture and I believed the Lord was comforting her and told her that her father would be ok. The next two days were spent on more door-to-door work and I had some good conversations.

We also had a visit from two ladies and when we told them that we were living by faith, they exclaimed, "Just like the disciples." They called back later with a gift for us to get some food. The Lord's provision once again.

On the Friday the team walked the coastal path into Port Stewart. I spoke out the words from the bandstand, from the gospel of John chapter 1, verses 1–14.

In the evening I telephoned Mary and she told me that she had read the words of the gospel of John, chapter 14, to her father, and he had confessed Jesus as his Lord and Saviour. HalleluYah! Praise the Lord!

This again is how the Lord will reveal to us His desire, that all who come to Him willingly, will be received and how the Holy

Spirit will speak to us to show us what to say, when we reach out to others. God still speaks to us today, through His word and through people that are obedient to Him.

The following day we were planning to visit a nightclub that evening and we found that it had been closed, due to a drugs raid. We returned to Port Rush later that day and had our evening meal at the Methodist Hall. At the pub later that evening I spoke with two ladies who were under the influence of alcohol. One of the team said I gave them the gospel very forcefully. We saw two more young ladies later and this team member showed his talent for patience and his ability to remember facts. He shared the gospel with these ladies and I encouraged him. We are all different and the Lord gives us differing gifts and talents, which we are able to use, if we choose to be willing and obedient.

On the Saturday we moved on to Ballymena Church. On the Monday we were invited to take part in a school assembly. Later that day we walked in a parade into the town.

We went on to another reception at the town hall where the mayor presented a plaque to Through Faith Missions, com-memorating the Walk Ulster mission. In the evening we went to a pub to share the gospel.

On the Sunday morning we took a bible class at Ballyloughan Presbyterian Church where I gave a children's talk and another team member gave the sermon. We had lunch at the Faith Mission Centre and went back to Ballyloughan Presbyterian Church for the evening service.

The following day I met two men who said that they were Calvinist's and after spending half an hour in discussion with them, I said that I had to get on to tell others that we are saved by grace alone, through faith alone, in Jesus Christ alone.

We had an appointment at a local factory to give a talk about the walk mission. One of the team gave his testimony and I spoke from 1 Corinthians chapter 10, verse 17. (For we, though many, are one bread and one body; for we all partake of that one bread.) and that we are charged to not to break up the body of Christ (the church). We were in a large warehouse type building and it was lunchtime.

At first no one seemed interested to hear, but men suddenly began to group around in a circle. We were given permission to spend as long as we wanted with the workforce and we had some amazing interesting conversations. Later, we were given a cheque to pay for our lunch and a second cheque towards the mission expenses. We were mightily blessed.

We continued visiting pubs to share the gospel in the evening. The next day we visited a school. When we arrived we suddenly discovered that we had two assemblies to cover.

After lunch we went into the shopping arcade. There was a main meeting in the town hall that evening and some of us were asked to go to the pub to share the gospel. On one occasion I asked the landlord if we could give a talk about the walk and sing a hymn. He said "Only if you sing my favourite hymns!" and then listed three! One of the patrons later took me to a local fish and chip shop to buy supper for all the team!

The next day we were given transport to Magheragall Church, Lisburn. In the evening we shared the gospel in the local pub.

The following day we had an unpleasant encounter with a local man who did not want us on his land and threatened us. We shook the dust off our feet and went back to the church after a couple of more calls. We had a time of prayer and gave this incident to the Lord.

Our team met up with the Rev. Peter Adams at lunchtime and he told us that anyone who was going to spend three weeks on the Mission, had to take the Friday off. During the afternoon the team continued the door-to-door visits.

As I was spending the three weeks on the Mission the next day (Friday), I spent the day by walking into Lisburn and hitch-hiked to Newcastle. I climbed Slieve Donnard mountain. As I was walking along the 'Mourne Wall' towards the peak of Slieve Donnard I was listening to a tape of praise music. I had not seen anyone for an hour, or more and the view was getting evermore spectacular, so I shouted a mighty "HalleluYah," and suddenly a head appeared above the Mourne wall and said "What's all this about the Walk of 1,000 Men?" I explained what the Walk was about and continued my walk to reach the summit. I then returned back to Newcastle and hitch-hiked back to Lisburn, arriving in time for the evening meal.

The next day (Saturday), I left my team to go back to Ballykelly church to join with my own church minister. He was in charge of ten teams of ten men and he had asked me to be his second-in-command for the final week.

On Sunday we went on to Willowfield Parish Church, where my minister preached at the morning service and also at the evening service. At 8.30p.m. the Salvation Army Band held a concert at the church.

The next day my minister and I went on to Rathcoole. I had some door-to-door work and went to the Bluefields Supporters Club. I had some good conversations there. We moved on to Strandstown Baptist Church on the Tuesday, sharing the gospel in the shopping precinct and also at the pub in the evening.

On the Wednesday we went on to Comber and had our lunch at the Methodist Church Hall. In the evening we went on to the pub to minister the gospel. On the Thursday I went door–to-door work and had some good conversations. I had lunch at the Methodist Church Hall and went door-to-door work again in the afternoon and again went to share the gospel in the local pub in the evening.

After a long three weeks of separation from my family and great experiences, both highs and lows, I was glad to be back home with my family. It had been an amazing experience.

Someone wrote in the Walk journal that in the middle of all the excitement, joy and hard work it was sometimes difficult for those involved to stand back for a moment and make an objective opinion. Many people were affected and responded to the gospel message.

After the mission finished the comment was made that the mission had made a very definite contribution to healing the divisions in Ulster. Praise the Lord.

CHAPTER SEVEN

Hartston Mission

Cambridge, Essex. March 1996

I had taken my car on this occasion, as it was a small mission. During our time of door-to-door work we found that there were many who were suffering and many who were ill. One person had been diagnosed with cancer, another was going through a marriage separation and another person was searching for more in life. We were able to pray for peace and for healing.

Many responded to the gospel message.

(In all the missions, people were given the opportunity to respond to the gospel call to repent and to receive Jesus Christ into their lives, as their Lord and Saviour.)

I heard that the evangelist (the Reverend Daniel Cozens) had been involved in a motor accident. I went to check that he was alright. He asked if I had anything prepared, as he was due to preach and he asked if I would go in his place. I did and a lady accepted Jesus Christ as her Lord, and Saviour. HalleluYah!

I met another lady who had been suffering from ME (Chronic Fatigue Syndrome) and she had been in a wheelchair. After she received prayer she had been able to walk about. HalleluYah! What an awesome God we serve!

In 1996, I was given the opportunity to buy a 3-year-old Land Rover Discovery. This was going to be very significant in 1998.

I returned home on the Saturday and on Sunday 14th April 1996 I was invited to preach at St. Johns, Chatham, Kent.

CHAPTER EIGHT

Walk Offa's Dyke

7th–29th September 1996

I had never been to Wales, let alone spoke Welsh and yet I was looking forward to this mission. I found that I had a cd by Noel Richards called The Event and this contained the worship song, Here is Love, Vast as the Ocean. Sue Rinaldi sung this in Welsh, on the cd, so I contacted Noel and he sent me the words in Welsh. After a lot of practise I learned the words phonetically and I sung the Welsh version when I visited Rhyl Baptist Church. It was a beautiful way to reach out to anyone who spoke Welsh. I also sang this hymn in Welsh, at a church in Rhosllanercrugog, or Rhos Wrexham.

Due to a computer crash at this time I lost my records of this Mission, so I am unable to give a factual account, but this was similar to the other missions with door-to-door work and prayer for any who needed it and people who responded to the gospel of Jesus Christ.

I returned from Walk Offas Dyke on the Saturday and on the Sunday I went to Rochester Cathedral where I was commissioned as a Diocesan Evangelist. I had begun the Developing Ministries Programme with the Anglican Church in 1990 for training as a Diocesan Evangelist. In January 1995, I was told that I was not going to be commissioned in the April of that year.

My belief is that the bible is the inspired word of God. It was suggested that I complete another year and then I would be commissioned.

There were also other similar missions. The Lord opened many doors, giving opportunities for the teams to share His love and faithfulness.

From October 1996 until May 1997 I was involved in the St. Francis Mission, Chatham, Kent. The Tendring Mission and The Key Mission, Haslemere.

After the Haslemere mission, I returned to Frensham Ponds with my Pastor, who baptised me. What an amazing experience this was! When we are baptised by full immersion it is an outward sign of our faith and we die to self, committing our life to our Lord and Saviour, Jesus Christ.

Jesus was baptised by full immersion.

(Matthew 3, verses 16,17).

When He had been baptized, Jesus came up immediately from the water; and behold, the heavens were opened to Him, and He saw the Spirit of God descending like a dove and alighting upon Him. And suddenly a voice came from heaven, saying, "This is My beloved Son, in whom I am well pleased."

The Lord continued to open many doors of opportunity to serve Him. At a Residential Home visit 5 people responded to the gospel call and asked Jesus to come into their lives and make them the people that He created them to be. Praise the Lord!

In the July of this year I was preparing for another busy week for the Yorkshire Wolds Mission.

I arrived at North Ferriby where I met up with the team and we walked to Welton and Melton. I was talking with two men in a local pub. One of them was from a Roman Catholic background. He had no sense of his sinful nature and therefore he felt that he had no need for repentance. (The bible says in Romans chapter 3, verse 23), "All have sinned and fall short of the glory of God."

On the Sunday morning at the 8.30 service I read the lesson from 1 Corinthians, chapter 13. The team took the service at 10.15 and in the afternoon there was a gardens open day. That evening I was invited by a Christian couple to dinner and an overnight stay at their home.

On the Monday I had door-to-door work and met with some challenges. One man said that he believed that there was death, then nothing. Two people were suffering from cancer. Another man's father was a Spiritualist. Another was an un-believer, but he took our Booklet, 'Knowing God Personally'.

That evening I went to have dinner with another Christian couple and I stayed with them the following evening as well. On the Tuesday the team had a school visit where we were invited to take part in the assembly. I had the afternoon to prepare for a Praise and Healing service, that I was to lead later.

On Wednesday we walked into South Cave and on the Thursday we had an invitation to another school and we took part in some lessons. In the afternoon we visited a Residential Home and in the evening we were invited to a men's group, where we enjoyed a meal and gave a talk about the walk mission. This was another of the Lord's provisions.

On the Friday we joined a Mum's and Toddlers group and went to the Family Centre for lunch. The afternoon gave us some free time for a shower, washing and enjoy a game of cricket, before continuing with our visiting the pubs to share the gospel.

On Saturday we continued with further door-to-door work and attended a garden Fete at Elleker Green. We had a meal and went to a house group in the evening.

On the Sunday we had a service at All Saints Church and in the afternoon we were transported on to West Lutton, Weaverthorpe, where we had further door-to-door work.

On the Monday there was a coffee morning, further door-to-door work in the afternoon and a pub visit to share the gospel, in the evening.

Tuesday saw more door-to-door work but this time we visited farms in the area.

On Wednesday morning I had an opportunity to ride a horse. I had never done this before and I was given a rosette for this 'first' as I had done well.

There was a lot of walking involved in the mission and in the afternoon of the Wednesday we walked into Sherburn. For the next two days we were on more door-to-door work in West Knapton and Sherburn.

The mission had to come to an end. It was amazing to see how God was using His servants and we were able to stretch our faith and use the spiritual gifts that He has given us for His praise and glory. Amen.

I returned home on the Saturday 7th September.

On the Sunday I preached at Kings Church, Rochester and I baptised my wife Mary at this service.

CHAPTER NINE

Sale of the Office

The Lord was at work once again in my life when in 1997 I began to feel restless in my business. The government began to bring in significant changes in giving insurance advice, resulting in a considerable cut in my commissions, this meant that I had to learn to trust God more.

After careful consideration and prayer, Mary and I came to the conclusion that we should sell the office, with the self-contained flat above. The Lord provided a buyer as our neighbour was interested in buying the property. This was another of the Lord's provisions as we did not even have to advertise it and this sale enabled us to be able to pay up the mortgage on our bungalow.

I set up an insurance scheme with an insurance broker to transfer my existing business to them and I was also able to introduce new customers. Furthermore I was able to offer people the gospel with the advertising literature for the scheme.

This freed me up to seek God who was preparing us as a family for what He had in store for us in the future.

From October to March I had some agency work.

In March I was introduced to an Evangelist. Mary and I prayed about this and sought the Lord, if it was His will for us. Our girls were getting older and more independent now. We believe God opened the door and I was thrilled to be part of that ministry, seeing more of the Lord working and using me to serve Him.

I had the Land Rover Discovery and I was able to travel around the country to go the churches and help them prepare for the meetings and also to collect the Evangelist and take him and assist him at these meetings.

I had stepped out in faith and although I was not paid an income, the Lord provided wonderfully. The churches gave towards my expenses, as I went ahead of the evangelist. I saw many come to faith and I also saw many miracles of healing.

On one occasion, I was at the home of a Pastor and I heard him opening and closing the cupboard doors in his kitchen. When he came out of his kitchen he had bags of food for myself and my family.

From this provision of the Lord, Mary and I set up a food ministry called 'Raven Ministries' and we supplied food hampers for the families who were struggling in our area and also we distributed them through the local churches.

These were exciting times, but after two years I could no longer afford to continue working with the Evangelist, I had to make a decision and that season came to an end.

This was a testing time for Mary and myself. It was a time of continuing to seek the Lord and waiting on Him for the next door to open for us.

We continued to supply the food hampers, they were such a blessing to those who received them.

CHAPTER TEN

The Lord's Provision

The Lord continued to provide gloriously, for me and my family. Our eldest daughter had told Mary and I that she wanted to get married. The Lord knew this and gloriously provided for us.

(Jeremiah chapter 29, verse 11.)
"For I know the thoughts that I think toward you, says the Lord, thoughts of peace and not of evil, to give you a future and a hope."

I was offered employment with a major construction company to work as an administrator in the finance department. I started employment with them on 20th March 2000. I was responsible to a Team Manager and the Finance Manager for the labour, plant and material costs, of a labour force of 120 people. This income provided for the forthcoming marriage of our eldest daughter.

Then on 24th September 2000 we had another celebration. Our youngest daughter, who had made a commitment to Jesus when she was eight years old, made a decision to be baptised. This took place at Temple Hill Baptist Church, in Dartford, Kent. Glory to God!

Marriage of our eldest Daughter on 16th August 2001

Our eldest daughter had told us that she wanted to get married and the couple chose Cooling Castle Barns, at Cooling in Kent, for the ceremony and wedding breakfast. On the 16th August 2001 we had a beautiful day and as a father, ordained by God, I was able to bless my daughter and son-in-law, in the wedding speech, with love, joy, peace, provision and friendship.

The contract with the major construction company was coming to an end and I was offered another contract in a different part of the country. This meant that I would be working away from home and my family. I chose not to accept this offer and therefore resigned on the 1st September 2001.

Another day of celebration was on 23rd October 2001 when we went to Greenwich University for the graduation of our middle daughter. This was a very special day for our daughter, as well as for Mary and myself.

I had been seeking God for the way forward and for a door to open in my life. In the meantime I obtained a position as a Materials Controller with a building company, and started on October 30th 2001. I was with this company until 29th February 2004.

On the 16th February 2002, whilst at work I received a telephone call to say that my sister was seriously ill and had been admitted to a hospital in the Medway Towns. I was able to get to see her just before she died. She knew the Lord and is with Him now.

Our second daughter's marriage 6th September 2002

Our second daughter announced that she wanted to get married and she chose Barbados. Mary and I travelled with our family to Barbados. There were thirteen of us in total and we had an amazing time. I had the privilege of walking my daughter down through the Flower Forest, to the sound of the wedding march played on steel drums. When we arrived at the dais, a minister handed me the Anglican prayer book. I shouted an almighty HalleluYah!

We had travelled all that distance and my daughter was married with the Anglican wedding service. Again, I was able to bless my daughter and her husband in my wedding speech with love, joy, peace, provision and friendship.

In 2003 we sold a property in France that we owned and had been renovating. Due to the fact that we did not even have to advertise it, this was another one of those 'God incidents.'

Another God incident was that I had been recommended for a position as a chaplain, with the Seamen's Christian Friend Society.

CHAPTER ELEVEN

Seamen's Christian Friend Society Chaplaincy

1st March 2004–29th March 2011

(Seamen's Christian Friend Society. Telephone 01625 610050, www.scfs.org)

I was invited to attend for an interview and Praise the Lord, I was successful and started an incredible time of working for them with seafarers from all over the world. The God we serve is an awesome God. I believe God had been preparing me for such a time as this from the years that I had spent in mission work previously and was the opening that I was waiting for, because this work was the most rewarding work that I have ever done and was another great leap of faith.

I visited seafarers on the many different Merchant Navy ships that came from all over the world, to the quay sides along 12 miles of the Lower River Thames and the mouth of the River Medway.

I found out where the various berths were, and had training to go into the Refinery and other areas that were extremely hazardous. I also obtained the various passes needed to gain access to the berths up and down the river.

On one ship I visited I took some of the crew, who came from India, to visit the sights in London. This was the first of many trips that I was able to arrange for the seafarers.

I also was able to distribute bibles in English and to some in their own language. I was following a tradition which is over one hundred and seventy years old.

I had the privilege of speaking with seafarers, mostly men, from Africa, America, Bangladesh, Benin, Brazil, Burma, (Myanmar), Canada, Cape Verde, China, Croatia, Denmark, Dominican Republic, Egypt, Estonia, Ethiopia, The Faroes, Finland, Georgia, Germany, Ghana, Goa, Greece, Holland, The Honduras, India, Indonesia, Iran, Israel, Japan, Kiribati, Korea, Latvia, Malaysia, Malta, Moldova, Montenegro, Norway, Pakistan, Panama, The Philippines, Poland, Romania, Russia, Senegal, Slovenia, South Korea, Sweden, Sri-Lanka, Thailand, Turkey, Tuvalo, Ukraine, United Kingdom, Vietnam and the Western Isles.

Many of these countries are affected by various disasters, Tsunamis, earthquakes, hurricanes, famine and drought. Ships are affected by piracy and terrorist activities.

I went on many different vessels including container ships, tankers, (gas and oil), cargo ships and cruise ships. I was required to wear safety equipment and had a number of inductions to go onto the jetties. Security was very tight, restricting the movement of seafarers, chaplains and port personnel.

Seafarers are away from home for long periods, up to a year at a time. They work long hours and often they cannot come off their ships due to work commitments. I called on them offering practical support, with telephone cards so that they could contact home. When some of the crew were free on a Sunday, they would let me know and I would drive to the ship, take them to Church and invite them back to our home where Mary would cook dinner for them, then I would take them back to their ship.

Some of the crew would want to visit the Seamen's Centre in the dock, where they were able to contact their families by telephone, or email.

I was able to distribute bibles to Indians in their native Hindi language and bibles and New Testaments to Filipino's in the Tagalog language and bibles in many other languages. I gave many the New King James version in English.

I also gave away 450 copies of United Christian Broadcasters 'The Word for Today' to the seafarers, every three months. (For more information about them visit www.ucb.co.uk)

The Holy Spirit opened up opportunities to occasionally hold services on board ship, sometimes including communion.

To help the seafarers in a practical way, I needed a multi-purpose vehicle and the opportunity arose for me to purchase a seven seater Toyota Lucida, at auction. Another of the Lord's provisions.

I was given the use of two rooms at a building inside the port at Tilbury Docks where I could store bibles, and gifts of knitted hats, as well as gifts of clothing, for seafarers. There was also a quiet area so that I could pray and minister to the seafarers.

I kept in touch with fellow chaplains around the world, by email advising them that a ship would be arriving and of the contacts that I had made on that ship.

The Lord was keeping me very busy.

I began to receive several invitations from churches to take services and to speak about my work with the seafarers. Through these church visits I was able to raise funds for the Seamen's Christian Friend Society and I also had the privilege of sharing the gospel message.

In April I went to Speldhurst Chapel, in Kent and also to Manor Mission in Laindon, Essex.

In May, I was invited to Socketts Heath Baptist Church in Grays, Essex, where I spoke on Psalm 107, verses 21–31. The Psalm states "O, that men would give thanks to the Lord for His goodness and for His wonderful works to the sons of men. Let them sacrifice the sacrifices of thanksgiving and declare His works with rejoicing."

It also refers to seafarers, those who go down to the sea in ships and tells of life on the sea.

I was also invited to St. Andrews in Chelmsford, Essex, where I spoke on Matthew chapter 25, verses 31–46, The Son of Man will Judge the Nations.

I spoke on this scripture because if we love the Lord we will want to please Him and that we are to use the talents that He has given us to help others to His praise and glory.

We are to feed the hungry and we will be fed the bread of life.

We are to give the thirsty a drink and we will receive the living water.

We are to clothe the naked and He will clothe us in righteousness.

We are to pray for the sick and they will recover.

We are to take the stranger in as we could be entertaining angels unawares.

We are to visit those in prison and we will see prisoners set free, not only those in prison but also those imprisoned by addictions to nicotine, alcohol, drugs, lust and materialism.

These things are able to be done through faith and it pleases God when we do them for His praise and glory.

How do we please God?

Through faith. Without faith it is impossible to please Him. (Hebrews chapter 11, verse 6.)

Please do not misunderstand me, I am not saying that you need to do good works to get into heaven. You do not obtain salvation through good works, but faith without works is a dead faith. We are not saved *by* works, but *for* works.

We are saved by grace alone, through faith alone, in Jesus Christ alone. Those who do not do the works that Jesus did, will hear those awful words, "Assuredly I say to you, inasmuch as you did not do it to one of the least of these, you did not do it to Me."

On the day of judgement, when we stand before Almighty God, we will find that there are two books in heaven.

One is the book of days in which all our days are written, (Psalms chapter 139, verse 16), and the other is the Lamb's Book of Life, (Revelation chapter 21, verse 27.)

Because we are all guilty and because all have sinned and fallen short of the glory of God, (Romans chapter 3, verse 23), we are all justly condemned and our punishment should be eternal damnation... But God, because of His awesome love for us has given us a way to escape our rightful condemnation and punishment.

Through accepting what Jesus Christ, our Redeemer and Saviour, has done for us, through His death on the cross and glorious resurrection, we will find that our names are written in the book of life. HalleluYah!

I meet many people who know about Jesus, but they do not know Him as their Lord and Saviour. They have head knowledge, but not heart knowledge of Jesus Christ.

Only those who have received God's solution to their sinfulness that is their disobedience towards God.

Only those who have repented of their old life and have turned from their old way of life and accepted Jesus as their Lord and Saviour, through what He did for us on the cross and dying in our place that we might live.

Only those who have turned back to God and said that they are sorry for their sin and received Him, will have their names written in the book of Life.

If Jesus Christ is not Lord of all, He is not Lord at all.

(Matthew chapter 25, verses 41–42). Jesus said to those who were on His left hand, the goats, "Depart from Me, you cursed, into the everlasting fire prepared for the devil and his angels: for I was hungry and you gave Me no food; I was thirsty and you gave Me no drink; I was a stranger and you did not take Me in, naked and you did not clothe Me, sick and in prison and you did not visit Me."

These are God's words from the bible. Today we have the choice to receive God's solution for our sinfulness – the free gift of God – the Lord Jesus and to ask Him into our life.

There is a prayer on page 118 that you can pray.

In June I returned to South Darenth Village Church, Kent, Thundersley Gospel Hall in Essex and Singlewell Road, Evangelical Church, Gravesend, Kent.

I was invited to Staplehurst Free Church where I spoke on The Emmaus Road, Luke chapter 24, verses 13–35.

In our reading we learn that two disciples were walking away from Jerusalem towards the village of Emmaus, which was seven miles distant. They were in total despair and in the depths of depression and devoid of hope. The Man for whom they had given up their occupations and followed for the past three years, had died. The Man that they had seen perform miracle after miracle. The Man that they believed had come to save them from the oppression of the Roman occupying forces. The Man that they had seen heal the sick by their thousands, feed people by the thousand, raise the dead, cast out demons and speak with such authority to the chief Priests, Scribes and the Pharisees that they asked "Who is this Man?" Where did He get his teaching?

The Man had told the disciples that He was the Messiah, the Christ, the Redeemer of Israel.

They had seen Him tried during the night, mocked, scourged, spat upon, punched, scourged with an instrument of torture that was nine leather straps, with stone and bone embedded that tore the flesh off His back and had a crown of thorns placed on His head. As His blood flowed, so the price for our salvation began to be paid.

They had seen the Roman governor, Pontius Pilate publicly wash his hands, saying that he found no fault in this Man.

They had seen Him crucified and when He was dead His body was taken and sealed in a tomb and a stone rolled across the entrance with Roman soldiers standing guard.

They were discussing these events and trying to reason why everything that they had hoped for, was lost.

They were depressed and devoid of hope.

Then we read that Jesus drew near to them. What an incredible statement that is!

Is there anything that you are going through today, leaving you in a similar situation, without hope?

When we reach the valley of despair, as we call on Him, Jesus will come alongside us.

Jesus said to them, "What kind of conversation is this that you have with one another as you walk and are sad? Cleophas replied, "Are you the only stranger in Jerusalem and have you not known the things that which happened there in these days?"

Jesus then asks them, "What things?"

So they said to Him, "The things concerning Jesus of Nazareth, who was a Prophet mighty in deed and word before God and all the people, and how the chief priests and our rulers delivered Him to be condemned to death, and crucified Him. But we were hoping that it was He who was going to redeem Israel. Indeed, besides all this, today is the third day since these things happened. Yes, and certain women of our company, who arrived at the tomb early, astonished us. When they did not find His body, they came saying that they had also seen a vision of angels who said He was alive. And certain of those who were with us went to the tomb and found it just as the women had said; but Him they did not see."

Then Jesus said to them, "O foolish ones, and slow to believe in all that the prophets have spoken! Ought not the Christ to have suffered these things and to enter into His glory?"

Jesus had said that He was going to die and be raised from the dead on the third day.

They did not realise that Jesus was the only one who was good enough to pay the price of our sin and our disobedience to God.

They had not begun to understand that He was the Christ, the Messiah and that He was the Son of God.

He was able to defeat sin and death and sickness and disease.

Jesus began at Moses and all the prophets and He expounded to them in all the scriptures the things concerning Himself.

We often lose sight of what our Lord showed us when He came into the world and we need to constantly go back to the scriptures to see how He showed us to live our lives. When Jesus died and rose again, He triumphed over principalities and powers, making a spectacle of them. (Colossians, chapter 2, verse 15.)

If we are to be used by the Lord, we need to know our position in Christ.

We are to love the Lord our God with all our heart, with all our soul and with all our mind.

We are also to love our neighbour as ourselves.

In God's eyes the greatest ability is availability.

We are to be willing and obedient to the Lord.

We read that Jesus made Himself known to the disciples in the breaking of bread, *after they had invited Him to stay*. (Verse 30)

Jesus will also make Himself known to us when we seek Him with all our hearts.

Later the disciples said, "Did not our hearts burn within us while He talked with us on the road and while He opened the scriptures to us?"

Do you want to open your heart to God and begin that relationship with the living Lord Jesus Christ now?

Today we have the choice to receive God's answer to our sinfulness – the free gift of God – to ask the Lord Jesus into our lives.

There is a prayer on page 118 that you can pray.

In the following years I was with the Seamen's Christian Friend Society and the Lord blessed the delivery of His word with three people making a confession of faith in the Lord Jesus and another fourteen people who re-dedicated their lives to the Lord.

I was invited to speak at two Churches in Essex and in this month I also returned to Singlewell Road Evangelical Church in Kent and gave a talk on Praising God every Day, based on Chronicles chapter 16, verses 8–36.

We are to give the Lord praise every day, for His goodness and His love and His mercy. Every day, not just on Sunday, because He is worthy of glory, worthy of honour and worthy of praise.

In this reading King David had just brought the Ark of the Covenant to Jerusalem.

King David was so filled with praise for God that he wrote this song of thanksgiving.

This is also recorded in the Psalms chapter 105, verses 1–15.

We are to declare the glory of the Lord, among the nations and His wonders among the peoples, for the Lord is great and greatly to be praised. (verses 24,25.)

We are to have a fear and an awe of God.

We are to respect God for He is Holy.

The god's (small g) of today, are idols. People today worship the idols of money, power and possessions. Nothing changes. People will look for a spiritual experience through sex, drugs and other New Age 'feel good' factors. These things are temporary, they do not last, and sadly people do not know the Lord, who created the Universe.

God's imagination is so immense that He could imagine the universe and then speak the Word, and the Holy Spirit put the stars into their allotted places.

Someone has said that the stars seem to have been flung into space!

We are to prepare ourselves to come before the Lord, because honour and majesty are before Him. Strength and gladness are in His place. Give to the Lord, O families of the peoples, Give to the Lord glory and strength (verses 27–29.)

We are to give to the Lord the glory due to His name.

We are to bring an offering and come before Him and worship Him in the beauty of holiness.

We are to give to the Lord the tithe, which belongs to God and then after that the offerings.

God gives us 100% and we are to return 10%.

If we are obedient to the Lord we inherit the blessings of Abraham. (Deuteronomy 28, verses 1–14.)

King David had been rejoicing. He did not have on his kingly robes and only had a linen ephod, or cloak. He was dressed like a common man and dancing was normally only done by women. Even more than this, he was dancing outrageously!!!

His wife Michal despised him. 1 Chronicles chapter 15, verse 29.

When people treat Christians with contempt they are treading on dangerous ground. Because Michal, King David's wife, was contemptuous of King David, she was barren. (2 Samuel chapter 6, verses 16–23.)

We must always remember that we have to forgive at all times, because we are forgiven. If we harbour unforgivingness, we allow the person that we have not forgiven to live 'rent free' in our lives. It is like a cancer that grows and will eventually destroy us.

The Lord is the righteous judge and He says, "Vengeance is Mine, I will repay." (Romans chapter 12, verse 19.)

We must also remember that Jesus was despised and rejected by men. A Man of sorrows and acquainted with grief. (Isaiah chapter 53, verse 3).

If you need help with unforgivingness, or anything else, you have the choice to come to God and receive His solution to your sinfulness – the free gift of God. You can ask the Lord Jesus into your life, to help you walk with Him.

There is a prayer on page 118 that you can pray.

I returned to Manor Mission in Essex and also to Thundersley Gospel Evangelical Church, Essex, where I spoke on Finding God's will, based on 1 Chronicles chapter 28, verses 1–10. In this reading King David had spoken with the prophet Nathan about building a temple for the Lord God of Israel.

God had told King David through the prophet Nathan, that David's heir would build the temple. (2 Samuel chapter 7, verse 12). This was because King David had been a man of war and had shed blood. (1 Chronicles chapter 28, verse 3.) King David then gives Solomon the plans for the vestibule, its houses, its treasuries, its upper chambers and the place of the mercy seat.

He continues to give instructions to build the temple exactly as he had been given, *by the Spirit of the Lord.* (2 Samuel chapter 28, verse 12.)

King David knew the Lord and he also knew that he had to be willing and obedient, to inherit all the blessings that God had for him, the blessings of Abraham.

If we seek the Lord He will come and guide us as we walk with Him.

He says that if we trust Him with all our heart and lean not on our own understanding and in all our ways acknowledge Him, He will direct our paths. (Proverbs chapter 3, verses 5,6).

You can find God's will for your life in His word, the Bible.

Today you have the choice to find God's will for you – to receive God's solution to your sinfulness – the free gift of God – to ask the Lord Jesus into your life and begin that relationship with Him.

I continued ship visiting and the Lord gave me opportunities to give away many bibles and encourage many of the seafarers to work through bible study courses.

There were times when situations became really difficult. I felt the enemy's attacks on the work that I was doing for the Lord.

I had to re-install Windows on my computer that had crashed. My hard drive was corrupted and I lost a large amount of information.

There were also days when I could not get across the Dartford Bridge, due to sheer weight of traffic, but I found that God was still at work behind the scenes.

In September I returned to Datchett Gospel Hall, East Berkshire, Chadwell Evangelical Church, Chadwell, Essex, and Riverview Methodist Church, Essex and St. Luke's Church, Cranham, Essex, where I spoke on Jeremiah chapter 8, verse 20.

In this scripture we read that, "The harvest is past, the summer is ended and we are not saved."

Jesus also spoke about a harvest in John chapter 4, verse 35, "Do you not say, 'There are still four months and *then* comes the harvest'? Behold, I say to you, lift up your eyes and look at the fields, for they are already white for harvest! And he who reaps receives wages, and gathers fruit for eternal life that both he who sows and he who reaps may rejoice together. For in this the saying is true: 'One sows and another reaps.' I sent you to reap that for which you have not laboured; others have laboured, and you have entered into their labours."

But God gave His word in Genesis chapter 8, verse 22. While the earth remains, seed time and harvest, cold and heat, winter and summer, day and night shall not cease.

God also said to the Israelites through Moses, and He says to us today in Deuteronomy chapter 8, verses 6–20, "Therefore you shall keep the commandments of the Lord your God, to walk in His ways and to fear Him. For the Lord your God is bringing you into a good land, a land of brooks of water, of fountains and springs, that flow out of valleys and hills; a land of wheat and barley, of vines and fig trees and pomegranates, land of olive oil and honey; a land in which you will eat bread without scarcity, in which you will lack nothing; a land whose stones are iron and out of whose hills you can dig copper. When you have eaten and are full, then you shall bless the Lord your God for the good land which He has given you.

"Beware that you do not forget the Lord your God by not keeping His commandments, His judgments, and His statutes, which I command you today, lest—when you have eaten and are full, and have built beautiful houses and dwell in them; and when your herds and your flocks multiply, and your silver and your gold are multiplied, and all that you have is multiplied; when your heart is lifted up, and you forget the Lord your God who brought you out of the land of Egypt, from the house of bondage; who led you through that great and terrible wilderness, in which were fiery serpents and scorpions and thirsty land where there was no water; who brought water for you out of the flinty rock; who fed you in the wilderness with manna, which your fathers did not know, that He might humble you and that He might test you, to do you good in the end—then you say in your heart, 'My power and the might of my hand have gained me this wealth.'

"And you shall remember the Lord your God, for it is He who gives you power to get wealth that He may establish His covenant which He swore to your fathers, as it is this day. Then it shall be, if you by any means forget the Lord your God, and follow other gods, and serve them and worship them, I testify against you this day that you shall surely perish. As the nations, which the Lord destroys before you, so you shall perish, because you would not be obedient to the voice of the Lord your God."

There are many today who trust in their possessions rather than in Jesus Christ.

Do we trust the Lord? Only those who know the Lord and do His will, know what His will is for their lives.

For a harvest to be gathered we must sow our seeds, our time, our talents and our finances.

So how are we saved?

We have to trust in the Lord Jesus Christ and say that we are sorry for our sin, our disobedience and ask Him to come into our lives and make us the person that He created us to be.

At this time there are many souls who need to know the Lord, both on the ships and also ashore.

Today you have the choice to receive God's solution to your sinfulness – the free gift of God and to ask the Lord Jesus into your life.

There is a prayer on page 118 that you can pray.

During October I went to one Church in Kent, one in Essex and one in North London. In November I was invited to three Churches in Essex and two in Kent.

At one of these Churches I spoke on Be Strong in Grace, 2 Timothy chapter 2, verses 1–13.

When I preached on this scripture I would ask:

1. Are you ready to fight for what you believe in?
2. Do you need more grace?

God is faithful.

We all have a past.

We all need a friend.

There is a Friend who is closer than a brother. (Proverbs chapter 18, verse 24).

Jesus Christ holds our future.

Paul tells Timothy in verse 2, "Be strong in the grace that is in Christ Jesus." He tells Timothy to commit the things that Paul has taught him, to faithful men who will then be able to teach them to others Timothy is also told that he must endure hardship.

Life is not easy for any of us.

Timothy is also told to be a good soldier.

What do soldiers do? They fight.

Paul goes on to state that no one who is engaged in warfare entangles himself with the affairs of this life, *that he may please the one who enlisted him.*

Who is Paul talking about pleasing?

Our Heavenly Father, Almighty God.

Paul then goes on to use the example of an athlete, who is not crowned, *unless he competes according to the rules.* We hear about athletes who cheat, by using drugs to enhance their performance. They are disqualified and dishonoured.

We need to honour God's rules; the Ten Commandments.

We are in a spiritual battle, continually.

Paul goes on to say, "Consider what I say, and may the Lord give you understanding in all things. Remember that Jesus Christ, of the seed of David, was raised from the dead, according to my gospel. For which I suffer trouble as an evildoer, even to the point of chains."

Paul continues, "But the word of God is not chained. Therefore I endure all things for the sake of the elect, that they also may obtain the salvation which is in Christ Jesus with eternal glory.

What hardships are you going through at this time?"

Do you need more grace?

Grace – God's riches at Christ's expense.

Getting what we do not deserve.

We are saved by grace alone, through faith alone, in Jesus Christ alone. So do you want to be strong in grace?

Receive the Lord Jesus as your Lord and Saviour. Ask Him to walk with you.

Ask Him to give you the grace to persevere.

In December I was again invited to speak at Emerson Park Evangelical Church in Hornchurch, Essex, and at South Darenth Village Church, Kent.

The Lord also blessed me with the opportunities to speak at churches and meetings, giving the gospel message of love and salvation and also for the opportunity for people to start a relationship with the Lord and in many instances I was able to pray for people.

I was privileged to give out bibles, bible study courses and bible notes to the seafarers and the Holy Spirit gave the opportunities to enable seafarers to begin a relationship with Jesus and receive Him as their Lord and Saviour.

CHAPTER TWELVE

The Pace Hots Up – 2005

It was a new year and I had now been with the Society for nine months. I continued to receive invitations to visit churches to speak and in January 2005, I went to Cliffe Christian Mission in Kent, South Park Chapel in Seven Kings, Essex, Wood Lane Baptist, Dagenham, Essex and Danbury Mission, Essex, where I gave the message on The Parable of the Talents, Matthew chapter 25, verses 14–30.

How do we use our talents to serve others and glorify God?

In this reading Jesus said that the Kingdom of heaven is like a man travelling to a far country, who calls his servants and delivers his goods to them, just before he leaves. We read that when the owner returns, he calls each servant to give an account for what he has done with the talents given to him. The one with five talents had made five more. He had put his talents to good use. Likewise the one with two talents had also put his talents to good use and made two more.

They are told, "Well done good and faithful servant, you were faithful over a few things, I will make you ruler over many things. Enter into the joy of your Lord." (verse 23.)

The one with one talent had buried his talent. He was afraid and had hid his talent. He was told that he was a wicked and lazy servant and what he had was taken from him and given to the one who had ten talents.

To those who have used their talents, the Lord says, "To everyone who has, more will be given and he will have an abundance; but from him who does not have, even what he has will be taken away. And He cast the unprofitable servant into outer darkness, where there will be weeping and gnashing of teeth."

We all have talents that the Lord has given us and, as Christians, we will be judged on what we have done with our lives on the Day of Judgement. (2 Corinthians chapter 5, verse 10.)

Of course we all want to hear the Lord say, "Well done good and faithful servant." To hear Jesus say this we need to please Him.

How do we please Jesus? Through faith. Without faith it is impossible to please Him. Hebrews chapter 11, verse 6.

Today you have the choice to receive God's answer to your sinfulness – the free gift of God – to ask the Lord Jesus into your life, to begin that relationship with God and be guided on how to use the talents and gifts to serve others and glorify God.

In the following years I was with the Seamen's Christian Friend Society and the Lord blessed the delivery of His word, with six people making a confession of faith in the Lord Jesus and another six people who re-dedicated their lives to the Lord.

I gave talks at Chadwell Evangelical Church in Tilbury, Essex, and Culverden Church in Tunbridge Wells, Kent. In February I was at Wood Lane Baptist Church, Dagenham, Essex, Upminster Baptist Church, Essex and Socketts Heath Baptist Church, Essex and Oxlow Lane Baptist Church, also in Essex. I had the privilege of baptising another seafarer this month.

In February, Mary and I were asked if we would host a Dutch Bible School student for a week as part of his training and he joined me on visits to the seafarers on the ships. We were invited to take a service on one ship and we celebrated communion with the crew. We visited a number of ships including container ships, tankers and cargo ships.

In March I was invited to take a service on a ship and I spoke on God's Everlasting Love, Romans chapter 8, verses 31–39.

I also shared this scripture and message at Cranmer Hall in Croydon, Surrey. During this month I also was invited to speak at Brewer Road Evangelical Church, Crawley, Sussex, Coleman Street Chapel, Southend, Essex, and Belhus Park Chapel also in Essex.

I had the privilege of baptising two more seafarers this month. Whenever I had this opportunity to baptise a seafarer there was a great deal of planning involved, sometimes months in advance. I had to check on when the ship would be due to dock and check that the ship had docked. There was a very quick turnaround period for the ships. I then had to get to the ship, make contact with the seafarer and take him to the venue for the baptism. Before this, I had to arrange a venue, either a church baptismal pool or a swimming pool, for the actual baptism. After the baptism I then had to get the seafarer back to the ship, before the ship sailed.

In April I was invited to speak at Broadlands Gospel Hall, Norfolk, Surrey Chapel, Norwich, Norfolk and Westcliffe Free Church in Essex.

In May and June I received invitations to speak at Churches in Essex and Kent.

Now it was July and we were halfway through the year. Mary and I booked a holiday in Italy, for a well-earned break.

When we returned home I had been re-invited back to give a talk at Thundersley Gospel Hall, in Essex.

In August I went to West Thurrock Chapel, Essex and I spoke at a thanksgiving service for one of our faithful ladies who had knitted many hats for the seafarers, at Staplehurst Free Church, Kent.

I was also invited to speak at a joint services meeting, at Westcliffe Free Church in Essex.

In September I went to four churches in Essex.

In October I spoke at Zion Baptist Church in Meopham, Kent and also at Socketts Heath Baptist Church in Grays Essex on The Parable of the Wise and Foolish Virgins, Matthew chapter 25, verses 1–13.

As I preached from this scripture I would ask.

Have you oil?

Are you ready?

The gospel is all about the sure hope that we have as believers in our Lord Jesus Christ that He gives us through His death and glorious resurrection.

In this parable Jesus is talking about the church being prepared for His return.

The church is described as the Bride of Christ. "For I have betrothed you to one husband that I may present you as a chaste virgin to Christ." (2 Corinthians chapter 11, verse 2).

In Matthew chapter 25, verse 1, reads, the ten went out to meet the bridegroom. The wise took extra oil *in their vessels.* (verse 4). The bridegroom was delayed.

There are some people today who do not believe that Jesus is about to return.

Some even think that they are good enough to stand before

God, even though they are living a life, which is disobedient to God.

At midnight a cry was heard, "Behold the bridegroom is coming, go out to meet him!" The virgins arose and trimmed their lamps. The foolish said, "Give us some of your oil, for our lamps are going out." The wise said, "No lest there should not be enough for us and for you, but rather go to those who sell and buy for yourselves." The foolish went to buy. The bridegroom came and those *who were ready* went in with him to the wedding and the door was shut.

When Jesus Christ returns we need to be ready.

I have found that there are people who have a knowledge of salvation, but do not live a life showing that Jesus Christ is Lord of their lives. They have head knowledge, but not a heart knowledge of Jesus Christ. They receive Christ but when tribulation, or persecution, or temptation, or tsunamis, or earthquakes, or terrorist bombs come, they fall away.

We find that the Ten Commandments are repeatedly broken, without repentance.

This is because there is no fear of God. Jesus is going to return one day. It could be today!

At midnight a cry was heard, "Behold the bridegroom is coming, go out and meet him!" Afterwards the other virgins came also, saying, "Lord, Lord, open to us!" But He answered and said, "Assuredly, I say to you I do not know you. Watch therefore, for you know neither the day, nor the hour in which the Son of Man is coming."

So are you ready for the return of the Lord? Have you asked Him to be Lord of your life? Today you have the choice to receive God's solution to your sinfulness – the free gift of God.

There is a prayer that you can pray on page 118.

To be prepared for His return, ask the Lord Jesus into your life.

I was interviewed in November on a Christian Radio Station, about my work as a Chaplain for the Seamen's Christian Friend Society and my work with the seafarers.

The Lord continued to open many doors to glorify Him and talk about my work with the seafarers from churches in Essex and Kent and I was also able to share the gospel message.

Many seafarers were eager to learn more about the Christian faith and I continued to be blessed as I gave out many bibles, bible study courses and bible notes, and the Holy Spirit continued to open up opportunities for me to lead a number of people to begin their relationship with Jesus and receive Him as their Lord and Saviour. I just had to be available for these people.

CHAPTER THIRTEEN

Our Vision 2006

The start of another year and the invitations continued to pour in. My diary was full. This was a truly blessed ministry.

In January I spoke at Sunnymeade Chapel in Billericay, Essex and returned to Wood Lane Baptist Church, Dagenham, Essex and Woolwich Baptist Church in Woolwich, London.

The Lord made a way for another seafarer to receive Jesus Christ as his Lord and Saviour. HalleluYah.

In February I went back to City Praise Centre in Gravesend, Kent, Thundersley Gospel Hall, Essex, Royston Evangelical Church, Hertfordshire and Welling Gospel Hall, Kent.

In March I spoke at Belhus Park Chapel in South Ockenden. By the grace of the Lord I had the privilege of baptising another seafarer this month.

I had more invitations to visit and speak from Churches in Kent and Essex. In May I was invited to speak at Catford

United Reform Church, Catford, London and Coney Hill Baptist Church in West Wickham, Kent.

In June I returned to speak at Manor Mission in Laindon, Essex, St. Paul's United Reform Church, Chalk Pentecostal Church and Milton Road Methodist Church, all in Kent.

I continued seeking the Lord for wisdom and guidance throughout. It was now March and I had a big birthday coming up. As a gift my family treated me to a flying lesson. I flew from Biggin Hill Airport to the Thames Crossing Bridge and along the Thames where I worked. I also flew over our home and also Chequers, the Prime Ministers country residence, returning to Biggin Hill airport, in Kent. This was an amazing experience, even more so considering I am not keen on heights! I received a certificate for my qualifying first flight. I am not quite a pilot yet, but we all have to start somewhere.

I was invited back to speak at a number of Churches that I had previously spoken at, in Essex, Kent and Sussex, from July to September.

During my visits to the churches I began to meet many affected by life from stress, burnout and depression and also from all the sickness and disease that the devil throws at us and Mary and I believe that the Lord was laying on our hearts the desire to sell our bungalow and buy a property that we could use to be a blessing to these people, so we wrote down our vision in September to have a property that we could use for this purpose.

This remained on our refrigerator for the next seven-and-a-half years, as we began to search for a property through five counties of England and also in Wales.

From October to December I received invitations from five Churches in Kent and eight in Essex.

Christmas was fast approaching. This was an extra busy time for the chaplains. I had many supporters from the Churches that supported the Society financially and who donated gifts of toiletries, knitted hats, scarves and gloves for Christmas presents for the seafarers. I included a New Testament in the parcels that I gave out. Mary and I and a group of volunteers would wrap the gifts.

During December I would distribute them to the seafarers as the ships arrived at the docks. The parcels and gifts were always appreciated by the seafarers. The knitted items especially, as it is extremely cold on the high seas.

On one occasion I was stopped by the police as I was walking along the jetty to the ship and the police checked the Christmas parcels in the sacks that I had with me.

The number of bible study courses that I gave out to seafarers increased this year.

The Holy Spirit opened up opportunities to pray for those who needed a healing touch from the Lord, as well as opportunities to lead many to receive Christ as their Lord and Saviour, both in the churches and amongst the seafarers. Glory to God.

In January 2007 I baptised another seafarer at West Thurrock Chapel. More invitations came and I was invited to speak at two Churches in London, one in East Berkshire and two in Kent.

In February I returned to Maldon Road Chapel, Maldon, Essex, City Praise Centre, Kent, Christchurch, Sidcup, Kent, and Riverview Methodist Church, Grays, Essex, giving a message on Breakfast by the Sea, John chapter 21, verses 1–14.

This talk I gave under the heading – Depression, Provision, Restoration and Preparation.

How do we get through the trials and battles that we face daily?

Do you feel that you lose too many battles? That the next wave might totally immerse you and overwhelm you?

The disciples, Simon Peter, Thomas, Nathaniel, the Sons of

Zebedeee and two others were depressed. They were totally in despair and in the depths of depression and devoid of hope. For the Man for whom they had given up their occupations and followed for the past three years had died. The Man that they had seen perform Miracle after Miracle. The Man that they believed had come to save them from the oppression of the Roman occupying forces. The Man that they had seen heal the sick by their thousands, feed by the thousand, raise the dead, cast out demons and speak with such authority to the chief Priests, Scribes and the Pharisees that they asked "Who is this Man?" Where did He get his teaching? The Man had told them that He was the Messiah, the Christ, the Redeemer of Israel. They had seen Him tried during the night, mocked, spat upon, punched, scourged with an instrument of torture that was nine leather straps with stone and bone embedded that tore the flesh off His back.

He was hung on a cross and He died. His body was taken and put in a sealed tomb with Roman soldiers on guard.

They were devoid of hope. They had doubts. Were they deluded? Simon Peter says, "I am going fishing." The others said, "We will go with you."

We have just got to do something.

That night they caught nothing.

They are feeling useless and worthless.

Are you feeling that way today?

Are you concerned about provision?

As they come near to the shore they see a Man. He says, "Children have you any food?"

How lovingly our Lord restores us.

When they say, "No," the Man says, "Cast your net on the right side of the boat and you will find some."

Suddenly, hope rose in their hearts, this was an echo of what they had experienced before. So they obediently cast and they were unable to draw in the net because it was so full of fish! John says, "It is the Lord." Simon jumps into the water and rushes to the shore. The rest came dragging the net full of fish. They find that the Man has a fire with fish and bread on it. He tells them to bring some of the fish that they had caught. There were one hundred and fifty three large fish in the net and the net was not broken. (Verse 11).

Jesus invites them to come and eat breakfast. None of the disciples dare ask, "Who are you?"– knowing that it was the Lord.

Jesus takes the bread and the fish and gives it to them. He then gently restored Peter, who had denied Him three times.

Today if you have doubts about who Jesus is, then ask Him to come into your life and reveal Himself.

In the following years that I was with the Seamen's Christian Friend Society the Lord blessed the delivery of this word and the Holy Spirit convicted ten people to make a confession of faith in the Lord Jesus and another twelve people re-dedicated their lives to the Lord.

In the next few months I returned to four Churches in Essex, Royston Evangelical Church in Hertfordshire, six other churches in Kent, one in Walthamstow, London and one in Norfolk.

I also returned to Broadlands Gospel Hall, Horning, Norfolk, and the message was on Where is Your Faith? Mark chapter 4, verses 35–41.

In this reading Jesus said, "Let us cross over to the other side."

He got into the boat and as they were crossing a great storm arose. Jesus was asleep in the stern of the boat. The disciples came to Him and woke Him saying, "Teacher do You not care that we are perishing?" Then Jesus arose, rebuked the wind and the waves saying, "Peace be still." And the wind ceased and there was a great calm. But He said to them, "Why are you so fearful? How is it that you have no faith? And they feared exceedingly and said to one another, "Who can this be that even the wind and the sea obey Him!"

As I presented this scripture I asked three questions:

1. Where is your faith?
2. Do you believe God?
3. Do you want to please God?

1. Where is your faith?

As you go through life you will experienced trial, tribulations and persecutions.

You can receive bad news and trouble comes.

A letter from the doctor.

Bank balance in the red.

Redundancy. Even the death of someone close to you?

Fear creeps in. Fear is a lack of faith in Almighty God.

There is a need to believe God. Not so much that God is on our side, but are we on God's side?

There is a need to stand alongside each other and encourage one another. Do not judge one another.

The bible says that we are to love the Lord our God with all our heart, with all our mind and all our strength and the second commandment is likewise unto it to love our neighbour as ourselves.

We are to trust God no matter what trials we are going through. Jesus said, "The thief comes to steal and to kill and to destroy, but He has come that we may have life and have it more abundantly." John chapter 10, verse 10.

2. Do you believe God?

People often accept Jesus, but when trials, temptation, tribulation, persecution, Tsunami earthquakes, piracy attacks, or terrorist bombings come, their love for the Lord grows cool.

God speaks to us in a still small voice but He shouts at us through our pain. We need forgiveness and also we need to forgive and to repent. (A change of mind. Saying sorry to God and turning away from our old way of life.)

Believing God.

Do we believe Him?

Jesus said, "Let us cross over to the other side." Verse 35. If Jesus is in the boat and He said it, then whatever is going on around us, we will get to the other side. HalleluYah!

3. Do you want to please God?

How do we please God? Through Faith. Without faith it is impossible to please God. (Hebrews chapter 11, verse 6).

We also need to be obedient and willing to be obedient.

In God's eyes each person is absolutely precious, incredibly special and totally unique and God would not have anyone perish.

How do we achieve fulfilment in all that God has promised us? By being obedient to His word. By accepting what He did for us by going all the way to the cross, dying in our place that we might have life abundantly and live with Him for eternity.

He paid the price that we could not afford, we owe a great debt.

We can do nothing to make ourselves more acceptable to God. We can only receive His goodness, love and mercy.

Do you want to accept Jesus Christ as your Lord and Saviour?

Do you want to have faith and believe Him and trust Him?

There is a prayer that you can pray on page 118.

During the time that I was with the Seamen's Christian Friend Society the Lord blessed the delivery of this word with seven people making a confession of faith in the Lord Jesus and another twenty-three people who re-dedicated their lives to the Lord.

I gave a talk at Hebron Chapel, Norfolk, on my work as a chaplain and I was invited back to Daws Green Church, Essex.

The remainder of the year I spoke at seventeen Churches in Essex, eight in Kent, one in Norfolk and two in London. During this period I also received my first invitation to speak at Rayners Lane Baptist Church in Harrow, Middlesex, where I gave a talk on The Emmaus Road, (Luke chapter 24, verses 13–35).

Our youngest daughter's marriage

On November 10th 2007 our youngest daughter was married at Chalk Pentecostal Church. The reception was held at Hempstead House, in Sittingbourne, Kent. Again, I was able to bless them with love, joy, peace, provision and friendship.

CHAPTER FOURTEEN
Speaking Engagements

I was now in my fourth year as a chaplain. I continued receiving many invitations to speak at churches about my work with the seafarers, on the ships that came to the berths along the River Thames and the River Medway and also to have an opportunity to share the gospel message.

In January 2008, I visited St Johns United Reform Church, in Orpington and spoke on the Parable of the Talents, Matthew chapter 25, verses 14–30.

In February I had a fuel leak on the Toyota Lucida, which required the seals being replaced in the fuel pump. This was a difficult job and I found a garage in Essex that specialised in these vehicles. I was able to get my car there and have the work completed.

The Lord provided a friend to help me.

I continued to travel to speak at Churches in Essex, Kent and Middlesex. I was invited to give a talk at Romford Evangelical

Men's Breakfast on Luke chapter 11, verses 5–13 "What is a Friend?"

In this scripture Jesus told a parable about a friend who called on his friend at midnight and asked for three loaves, because a friend had called on him.

He said, "Do not trouble me; the door is now shut. I cannot come to the door and give to you." He does not want to get up and help. But Jesus said because of his persistence he will get up and give him as many loaves as he needs.

A true friend is someone who is prepared to be inconvenienced.

God is interested in the small things in our lives. I needed a friend and the Lord provided for me. I had a knee problem and I was unable to walk any distance. My car was booked in at a garage in Essex for 8.00 a.m. I phoned a friend who said that he would meet me at the garage. He came and took me out to breakfast and then took me on to a Pastor's home for the day. Later he collected me and we found that the car was still not ready, so he took me to the ferry so that I could get back to Gravesend, in Kent. He called on me the next day at my home in Kent and took me back to Essex, where I was able to collect the car. Two good friends.

We all have a past, we all need a friend, but there is a friend who is closer than a brother. (Proverbs chapter 18, verse 24.)

His name is Jesus.

Do you know that God is faithful and wants to be your friend?

Do you know Jesus?

Do you have a personal relationship with Him?

The bible contains the greatest mystery and the greatest adventure.

Jesus said in John chapter 15, verses 11–17; "These things I have spoken to you, that My joy may remain in you, and that your joy may be full. This is My commandment, that you love one another as I have loved you. Greater love has no one than this, than to lay down one's life for his friends. You are My friends if you do whatever I command you. No longer do I call you servants, for a servant does not know what his master is doing; but I have called you friends, for all things that I heard from My Father I have made known to you. You did not choose Me, but I chose you and appointed you that you should go and bear fruit, and that your fruit should remain, that whatever you ask the Father in My name He may give you. These things I command you, that you love one another."

Jesus left the glory of heaven to come to earth and to die on the cross for you and for me. To pay the price that a righteous God demanded for our sin, our disobedience.

The issue is that we all have free will.

We can either go God's way, or our own way.

Do you need a friend to help you?

Maybe you once had a passion for Jesus, but your love for Him has cooled? Maybe you have walked away from the Lord?

God wants to welcome you back, because of His love for you. Today you can choose to return to the Lord and go His way.

You will find a prayer on page 118 to help you.

I returned to five Churches in Essex, one in Altringham, Cheshire and one in Kent.

In one of these churches I gave a talk on the Raising of Lazarus, John chapter 11, verses 1–44. In this reading Mary and Martha had sent to Jesus saying, "Lord, behold he who you love is sick." (Verse 3.) Jesus then said, "This sickness is not unto death, but for the glory of God, that the Son of God may be glorified through it."

Now Jesus loved Martha and her sister and Lazarus. Jesus had left Jerusalem, in Judea, because they had sought to seize Him. (Verse 39.) They were going to kill Him (verse 8) but His hour had not yet come.

Now Jesus says, "Let us go to Judea again." Jesus said to them plainly, "Lazarus is dead." Then Jesus says, "I am glad for your sakes that I was not there, that you may believe. Nevertheless let us go to Him."

Thomas (who we tend to remember as the doubter, John chapter 20, verses 24–29) is prepared to die for our Lord and shows great courage when he says, "Let us go and die with Him." (Verse 16).

Martha heard that Jesus was coming and went to meet Him. She says, "Lord, if You had been here, my brother would not have died. But even now I know that whatever You ask of God, God will give You." Jesus said, "Your brother will rise again." Martha replied, "I know that he will rise in the resurrection on the last day."

Jesus then says, "I am the resurrection and the life. He who believes in Me, though he may die, he shall live. And whoever believes in Me shall never die. Do you believe this?" Now Martha declares, "Yes Lord, I believe that You are the Christ, the Son of God, who is to come into the world."

Jesus then goes to the tomb.

When He saw the grief of the people He groaned in His spirit and was troubled. (Verse 33.)

Jesus is offended when the Devil robs us of our joy!!!

He asks, "Where have you laid him."

They said to Him, "Lord come and see."

Then we read that Jesus wept.

Then, again groaning in Himself, He came to the tomb and He tells the people to take away the stone. Martha says, "There will be a stench, for he has been dead for four days." Jesus said, "Did I not say to you that if you would believe you would see the glory of God?" Then He said, "Father I thank You that You have heard Me, and I know that You always hear Me, but because of the people standing by I said this, that they may believe that You sent Me." Then Jesus said, "Lazarus, come forth!" And he who died came out bound hand and foot with grave clothes, and his face was wrapped in a cloth. Jesus said to them, "Loose him and let him go."

Are you bound by circumstances and events?

Today Jesus wants you to be loosed and set free.

During the next three months I went to two Churches in Kent and one in Essex.

In June, Mary and I had a 'busman's holiday' where we went

to Norfolk and while we were there I had arranged to speak at Mundesley Free Church, for three meetings, Brook Hall, Sherringham and Surrey Chapel, Norwich.

I was also invited to speak at Dry Street Memorial Chapel, Essex, Woolwich Central Baptist Church, Woolwich, London, Also at West Road Church, Bury-St-Edmunds, where I gave a message on The Good Shepherd, (John chapter 10, verses 7– 18).

In this reading Jesus said, "Most assuredly, I say to you, I am the door of the sheep. All who ever came before Me are thieves and robbers, but the sheep did not hear them. I am the door. If anyone enters by Me, he will be saved, and will go in and out and find pasture. The thief does not come except to steal, and to kill, and to destroy. I have come that they may have life, and that they may have it more abundantly."

The Devil is a thief that comes to steal and to kill and destroy.

But Jesus has come that we may have life and have it more abundantly. (John chapter 10, verse 10.)

Abundantly means superabundance, excessive, overflowing, surplus, over and above, more than enough, profuse, extraordinary, above the ordinary, more than sufficient.

Is your life like this today?

Jesus said, "I am the good shepherd. The shepherd gives his life for the sheep, but the hireling, he who is not the shepherd, *one who does not own the sheep,* sees the wolf coming and flees.

The hireling flees because he is a hireling and does not care about the sheep. (Verse 13.) Jesus said, "I am the good shepherd and I know My sheep and I am known by My own. As the Father knows Me, even so I know the Father and I lay down My life for the sheep. *Other sheep I have, which are not of this fold, them also I must bring and they will hear My voice and there will be ONE FLOCK and one shepherd."*

Jesus then said, "Therefore My Father loves Me."

Jesus said, "Therefore My Father loves Me. Because I lay down My life that I may take it up again. No one takes it from Me, but I lay it down of Myself. I have the power to lay it down and I have the power to take it up again. This command I received from My Father."

Do you want to know the person of Jesus Christ and to be able to enjoy this abundant life?

Then call on the name of the Lord. Seek Him while He may be found.

You will find a prayer to help you on page 118.

You will not suddenly find that life becomes easy.

You will need to join a church for fellowship, teaching and guidance.

In the evening I went to West Road Church, Bury-St-Edmunds and spoke on my work as a chaplain at their Missions event.

In the following years that I was with the Seamen's Christian Friend Society the Lord blessed the delivery of this word with two people making a confession of faith in the Lord Jesus and another person who re-dedicated their life to the Lord.

I returned to Sawyers Church, Chelmsford, Essex, Shirley Road Gospel Church, Enfield, Manor Mission, Laindon, Essex, Coleman Street Chapel and Southend Evangelical Church, Southend-on-Sea, Essex.

I was invited to Bulford Evangelical Church, Bulford, Wiltshire to speak at both morning and evening services and also to Oakhall Church, Caterham, Surrey, four Churches in Kent, four Churches in Essex and one in London.

I received an invitation back to Socketts Heath Baptist Church, Grays, Essex, and gave a message on God's Love for His People, Hosea chapter 11.

The background to this story is that God told Hosea to marry Gomer who was a harlot (prostitute). Gomer was unfaithful and left Hosea, but every time that she left him Hosea had to go after her and get her back.

This was an example of God's love for us. He knows what it is like to be in a relationship where there is rejection and a spouse is unfaithful.

God is passionate about us. He has incredible love for us and He mourns when we reject Him.

God is showing His love for us and saying that despite our betrayal of Him, He remains faithful.

The greatest example of His love for us is when Jesus came to this earth as a man, laying aside His majesty and going to the cross, to die on that cross and pay the price that a just God required for our salvation and restoration.

Only those who have received God's solution to their sinfulness, that is, their disobedience towards God, can be saved.

Only those who have repented of their old way of life, that is, those who have turned from their old way of life and have accepted Jesus as their Lord and Saviour, accepting what He did for us, dying in our place, that we might live, can know of His salvation for us.

Only those who have turned back to God and said that they are sorry for their sin and received Jesus Christ as their Lord will have their names written in the Lambs book of life.

Do you want to receive God's solution to your sin?

You will find a prayer that you can pray on page 118.

In November and December I spoke at three Churches in Essex and two Churches in Kent. During the year I was invited to a church ladies meeting, where a lady came up to me afterwards and said that she had a pain in her knee. I prayed with her and two weeks later she telephoned me to say that she had not had any pain since the prayer. Praise the Lord.

The Holy Spirit continued to provide opportunities for me to pray for those who were unwell and also opened a door to lead some to receive Jesus Christ as their Lord and Saviour, both in the churches and also with the seafarers.

CHAPTER FIFTEEN

Speaking Engagements

I was still being incredibly blessed with all the invitations that I received to speak at Churches across the country.

In 2009, I continued to travel to the counties of Kent, Essex, Berkshire and Norfolk with twenty seven other invitations.

Mary and I also had a surprise invitation to attend the garden party at Buckingham Palace, as a chaplain of the Seamen's Christian Friend Society, so we went shopping for a new outfit for Mary and with our passes safely in our possession we made our way to Buckingham Palace on the 7th July. We had a great day, enjoying the amazing surroundings, delicious food, plus the grandeur of the occasion. There was a huge thunderstorm but even this did not dampen our enjoyment of the day. We made the most of our day in London and found an Italian restaurant, where we went for a meal in the evening, before heading home.

I continued with twenty six further speaking engagements at Churches in Kent, Essex and London.

The Holy Spirit opened up more opportunities to pray for people that had various needs and He also gave openings to lead people in prayer to receive Jesus Christ as their Lord and Saviour.

I also had many more opportunities to give out bibles, bible notes and bible study courses, to the seafarers.

Another year had passed and there were many more doors of opportunity that the Lord opened to serve the seafarers, along with invitations to speak at even more Churches across the country.

In January 2010 I went to Royston Evangelical Church and gave a message on Glory in the Highest, Luke chapter 2, verses 8–20.

I would ask people "Are you ready for the suddenlies of God?

Jesus Christ left the glory of heaven to come to the earth to die for our sins, our disobedience, so that we may have life and have life more abundantly.

He came to ordinary people.

He came as a baby.

Joseph and Mary, a Jewish couple who were betrothed, a pre-marriage contract. Mary was pregnant, but Joseph was not the father. The Jews had a punishment for adultery, a sentence of death by stoning. Joseph was a just man. He had a mind to put away Mary quietly.

But God... an angel had visited Mary. Luke chapter 1, verses 28–38.

Matthew chapter 1, verses 21–25, The angel also came to Joseph, verses 20,21, But while he thought about these things, behold, an angel of the Lord appeared to him in a dream, saying, "Joseph, son of David, do not be afraid to take to you Mary your wife, for that which is conceived in her is of the Holy Spirit. And she will bring forth a Son, and you shall call His name Jesus, for He will save His people from their sins." So Joseph did as the angel commanded him and took to him his wife and did not know her until she had bought forth her first-born Son. And he called His name Jesus. Matthew chapter 1, verses 24,25.

The angel also came to the shepherds.

Now these shepherds were working through the night. They were not held in great esteem. They were keeping watch when an angel of the Lord stood before them and the glory of the Lord shone around them **and they were greatly afraid.**

These men were not acceptable to give evidence in a court of law as witnesses, because they were considered unreliable.

But God... used them to herald the most incredible news for the hope of mankind.

The angel of the Lord said to them, "Do not be afraid, for behold I bring you good tidings of great joy, which will be to all people. For there is born to you this day in the city of David, a Saviour who is Christ the Lord. And this will be the sign to you. You will find a Babe wrapped in swaddling clothes, lying in a manger."

And then... suddenly there was with the angel a multitude of the heavenly host praising God and saying, "Glory to God in the highest, and on earth peace, goodwill towards men."

Let me tell you that God is a God of the suddenlies.

The shepherds said, "Let us go to Bethlehem to see this sight." When they had seen Him, they made it widely known, the saying that had been told them concerning this Child.

Christ the Saviour was born. HalleluYah.

Do not miss the day of visitation.

Be ready for the suddenlies.

Jesus is coming again.

Are you ready to believe God?

Have you received Jesus as your Lord and Saviour?

In the time that I was with the Seamen's Christian Friend Society the Lord blessed the delivery of this word with one person making a confession of faith in the Lord Jesus and another nine people who re-dedicated their lives to the Lord.

For the next three months I had seven invitations to speak at Churches in Kent and Essex. At one of them I spoke on John chapter 3, verses 1–21, You must be Born Again.

In this reading Nicodemus came to Jesus at night. He was a teacher of the law, a Pharisee. He did not want to lose his position of authority, but he wanted to find out more about Jesus. He said, "Rabbi, We know that You are a teacher come from God, for no one can do these signs that You do unless God is with Him." Jesus answered, "Most assuredly, I say to you, unless one is born again, he cannot see the Kingdom of God." Nicodemus then asks, "How can a man be born when he is old?" Jesus replies, "Most assuredly, I say to you, unless one is born of water and the Spirit, he cannot enter the Kingdom of God."

Jesus later says these beautiful words for the hope of mankind, "For God so loved the world that He gave His only begotten Son, that whoever believes in Him shall not perish but have everlasting life. For God did not send His Son into the world to condemn the world, but that the world through Him might be saved."

So where do you stand today? Are you for God or against Him?

It is not so much that God is on our side, but whether we are on God's side, or not?

Jesus goes on to say, "He who believes in Him, is not condemned; but he who does not believe is condemned already, because he has not believed in the name of the only begotten Son of God. And this is the condemnation, that the light has come into the world, and men loved darkness rather than light, because their deeds were evil."

So do you believe God, or not, today?

Have you a relationship with the living Lord Jesus Christ?

This day choose life.

Further Church invitations took me to Enfield, Middlesex, Danbury Mission, Danbury, Essex, Socketts Heath Baptist Church, Essex, Salisbury Road Baptist Church, Grays, Essex and Westcliffe Free Church, Essex. In May and June I returned to three Churches in Essex, two in Kent and one in East Berkshire.

I had been studying a Counselling Skills Course and in June 2010, I passed the exam and received the AQA Intermediate Certificate for Counselling Skills.

For the next three months I went to speak at five churches in Essex, Kent and Enfield. In October there was an invitation for all the chaplains to attend a Conference at All Saints Pastoral Centre in London. As I was about to leave home I received a telephone call from a shipping agent, requesting that I attend a ship where a seafarer had died. All the chaplains had left for the Conference, so I visited the ship. The crew were traumatised by the incident, but still had to carry on their work. I was able to minister to them.

I was invited back to Oxlow Lane Baptist Church, Dagenham, Essex, where I spoke on You are not alone, John chapter 16, verses 25–33.

Two thousand years ago a Man called Jesus lived on this earth. Jesus worked with Joseph, who was a carpenter. He was very fit. He had to be. He worked on the cedars of Lebanon. He had to cut this hard wood with an axe. He was also very strong.

We read in the bible that He was tried during the night. He was punished with 39 lashes of an instrument of torture. Nine leather thongs with stone and bone embedded, that tore the flesh off His back.

After this He carried His cross. He was then crucified.

While He was alive Jesus spoke with authority. When tempted by the Devil in the wilderness, to command the stones to become bread, after forty days of fasting, Jesus said, "Man shall not live by bread alone, but by every word that proceeds from the mouth of God." Matthew chapter 4, verse 4.

When the Devil said, "Throw Yourself down from the temple because He shall give His angels charge over You," Jesus said, "It is written, you shall not tempt the Lord your God. When the Devil offered Jesus the kingdoms of the world and their glory, Jesus said, "Away with you Satan! For it is written, you shall worship the Lord your God, and Him only you shall serve." The chief priests and the scribes and the Pharisees asked Him questions and were astonished at His teaching, along with all the multitudes. Matthew chapter 22, verse 33.

He said that He was the Messiah, the Christ, the Saviour of the world. He also said that He would die and that He would rise again on the third day. Matthew chapter 20, verse 19.

You may have received the call to give your life to Christ.

This does not mean that you will suddenly be immune from the troubles of this world.

We must keep the faith if we are to become the person that

God intended each one to become.

I do not believe that we can lose our salvation, but we have free will and we can walk away from it.

If we walk away from God and deny that Jesus died for our sins and our disobedience, then God will let us go our own way.

We have free will and therefore if we want to live God's way we must always choose to be obedient to God.

If we continue to choose to live a lifestyle that is not what God intended for us, then we will find on the day of judgement that God will say, "I do not know you."

If we believe that Jesus Christ died for us and we receive Him into our lives, we are believing God and His plan for us. But if we do no more than that, we can find ourselves being tempted back into our old ways.

Why is this? It is because there is a Devil and he is a liar and a cheat and a thief, who comes to kill and to steal and to destroy. But Jesus has come that we may have life and have it more abundantly. John chapter 10, verse 10.

Have you invited Jesus into your life?

There is a prayer to help you on page 118.

I spoke at nine other churches in Kent and Essex over the next two months. On Remembrance Sunday I went to Culver Evangelical Church, Stanmore, Middlesex and spoke on Great Love, John chapter 15, verses 9–17.

In the reading Jesus said, "As the Father loved Me, I also have loved you; abide in My love. If you keep My commandments, you will abide in My love, just as I have kept My Father's commandments and abide in His love. These things I have spoken to you, that My joy may remain in you, and that your joy may be full. This is My commandment, that you love one another as I have loved you. Greater love has no one than this, than to lay down one's life for his friends. You are My friends if you do whatever I command you. No longer do I call you servants, for a servant does not know what his master is doing; but I have called you friends, for all things that I heard from My Father I have made known to you. You did not choose Me, but I chose you and appointed you that you should go and bear fruit, and that your fruit should remain, that whatever you ask the Father in My name He may give you. These things I command you, that you love one another."

I continued by saying that on Remembrance Sunday we remember those who have given their lives to make this world a better place to live in. We have much to be thankful for.

Many gave their lives selflessly, but there are also many who live their lives selfishly today.

We are in a society in which lawlessness abounds and people choosing to live lifestyles that do not honour the living God.

We see fear and anger today.

Young people carrying knives and guns.

There is no respect for authority.

Many break the Ten Commandments and there is no repentance.

There is no fear of God.

People do not believe in Jesus.

There is disobedience towards Almighty God.

Aids is rampant, but this seems to have been forgotten.

Also 50 years of the abortion act, with tens of thousands of innocents murdered each year.

It cost God the suffering and death of Jesus Christ to redeem us from our sin.

We need to seek the Lord and revive our passion for Jesus Christ, to proclaim His death and glorious resurrection, but the Lord knew this would happen.

2,000 years ago He came to this earth. He laid aside His majesty to come and be born of a virgin. He came to pay the ultimate sacrifice that a just God required for our salvation. He said that He was the Messiah, the Christ, the Saviour of the world.

When He was thirty years of age, He went around healing the sick, and feeding the hungry. He raised the dead and spoke with such authority that the Chief Priests and the Scribes and the Pharisees said, "Who is this Man, and from where does He get His teaching?"

When He was thirty-three He was taken by evil men and tried during the night. He was mocked. He was punched. He was derided. He was whipped and he was scourged. He had a crown of thorns placed on His head. And as He begun to shed His blood, the price for our disobedience began to be paid.

As He hung on that cross He said, "Father forgive them, for they know not what they do."

Then He said, "It is finished," and He gave up His Spirit and died, triumphing over sin and death, sickness and disease.

He wiped out the handwriting of requirements against us, which was contrary to us. And He has taken it out of the way, having nailed it to the cross. Having disarmed principalities and powers, He made a public spectacle of them, triumphing over them in it. Colossians chapter 2, verses 14–15.

The veil in the temple was torn in two from top to bottom, graves were opened and many bodies of the saints who had fallen asleep were raised.

He set the captives free. Matthew chapter 27, verses 51, 52.

He rose from the dead on the third day, and He is alive today.

HalleluYah!

So do you know this Jesus?

There were six further speaking engagements at Norfolk Churches, plus three in Kent and one in London.

In March 2011 I reached retirement age and I had to accept that this season in my life had come to an end and sadly, I had to walk away from this amazing work.

I took up my pension and discovered that if I had left it any longer I would have lost the benefit of a guaranteed annuity. (This was the best type of pension available and was going to be a great asset to me for the vision that Mary and I had in September 2006).

There now followed a time of waiting on the Lord. I had been incredibly busy and suddenly everything stopped, but God was preparing us for our next step.

CHAPTER SIXTEEN

Further Testing

My doctor had given me a cardiac test and asked that I went for further tests. I had an appointment on 20th January 2012 at Kings College Hospital for a Cardiac Stress Echo test. I told the consultant that I would take the test but I would not have any operations, as there was nothing wrong with me. (I had recently returned from climbing Mount Snowdon, in North Wales.)

I was on the treadmill for 10 minutes and getting out of breath, so the operators said that I could stop. After perusing the results and asking if I had any pain, when I told them that I had no pain, he said that he had seen this before and that it was a false positive! If I had gone another two minutes on the treadmill, I would have completed the airline pilots' fitness test! Glory to God.

The Lord's hand for Mary and my future provision were being formed. Our vision became a step nearer.

CHAPTER SEVENTEEN

The Lord's Providence and our Vision Fulfilled

Mary and I continued our search for a property and in January 2014 we were in Wales to view three properties. We were travelling at 70 mph and had a front offside tyre blow out. Our guardian angels were working overtime! Mary and I were unharmed. Praise the Lord for His protection.

A road spring had collapsed and punctured the tyre. We had the car towed to a garage where it was repaired the same day, but we did not know this, as we hired a car and went on to the B&B that we had booked into. We had no mobile phone signal. We had rescheduled our viewings and went to view The Rectory, in Brechfa, the next day, along with the other two properties.

We found that The Rectory totally suited our vision. By the grace of God, our offer was accepted and we moved in on 28th April 2014. HalleluYah.

We were not permitted to retain the name "The Rectory" so we changed the name to "Emmanuel". This means "God with us."

The main property was built around 1880 with an extension to the ground and first floors adding a lounge and a kitchen on the ground floor and three bedrooms on the first floor and there was also an extension to the North West corner where the original bathroom was. This extension was completed around 1990.

We had a new kitchen installed and we decorated the utility room. We decorated the room used as our lounge. We had three en suites installed in the letting rooms and converted the toilet into another en suite, on the ground floor, decorating that ground floor room, as a bedroom.

We also took out the bath and had a walk in shower installed and added another toilet and replaced the original toilet in the wc.

After taking out the old fireplace in the guest lounge, we found there was room to install a multi-fuel stove and this is now an inglenook fireplace.

We also have a guest dining room where we can serve up to twelve people.

We then had a French drain installed at the Northern end of the property and also had the pathway stepped to make it safer to negotiate.

There are beautiful views surrounding the property with some splendid walks nearby.

It is very peaceful most of the time.

Our home is used for the glory of God and we minister to people. There is also a bible and a copy of United Christian Broadcasters 'The Word for Today' in every room. (For more information about them visit www.ucb.co.uk)

In 2016, I was at the Bible College of Wales on the day before the referendum for leaving Europe and there was a prophecy given that we would leave the European Union.

The Bible College of Wales is where Rees Howells (Intercessors for Britain) met with others, to pray for Britain during World War 1 and World War 2 and the Lord intervened to save this nation.

Mary and I were part of the Mission to Wales, between 6th to 15th July 2017, it was amazing seeing God at work across Wales in 9 days. Each day one hour was spent evangelising, following an hour of praise and worship. 3350 people responded in the nine days and prayed to receive Jesus Christ as their Lord and Saviour. Glory to God. HalleluYah. (Mission to Wales: www.newwinecymru.co.uk)

Mary and I are very blessed and we have three wonderful sons-in-law who are married to our three daughters. They have given us five beautiful grandchildren, three girls and two boys.

I continue to be used by the Lord, both at home and in our home church. I evangelise and take the gospel to people on the streets in Carmarthen. I continue to be used by the Holy Spirit to lead people to the Lord and also to pray for the sick.

The Lord remains faithful. I pray that God will continue to use me in the remaining years of my dash and that I will be available for Him and remain faithful to His call.

The bible tells us that the Lord will return to the earth again one day and we will all be judged by Him. The only way that we can stand before Almighty God is to receive Jesus as our Lord and Saviour.

We all need a friend and there is a friend who is closer than a brother. Jesus knows our past and is ready to forgive and accept us. You can begin that relationship with Jesus today by repenting and confessing your sins to Him and asking Him to come into your life.

Here is a prayer that you can pray

Dear Lord Jesus,

I thank You, for dying on the cross for me. I am sorry for my sin, and my disobedience to You. Thank You, that You rose from the dead, defeating sin and death and sickness and disease and now pray for me from heaven. Forgive me Lord and I ask You to come into my life and help me, through Your Holy Spirit, to live for You and be the person You created me to be. Amen.

If you have said this prayer and meant it, I encourage you to find a bible-based and Christ centred church to gain support and encouragement from other believers, in your journey with the Lord.

You will need to be encouraged to read the word of God every day so that you can find guidance and wisdom on how to lead a Christ centred life.

You will also need to be baptised and show the world that you have decided to follow the Lord.